Don t Get MAD... Write!

Don't Get MAD... Write!

BRUCE WEST

Stoddart

Copyright © 1992 by Bruce West

First published in 1992 by
Stoddart Publishing Co. Limited
34 Lesmill Road
Toronto, Canada
M3B 2T6

Canadian Cataloguing in Publication Data

West, Bruce, 1951–
Don't get mad . . . write!

ISBN 0-7737-5487-3

1. Consumer complaints.   2. Letter-writing.   3. Complaint letters.
I. Title.

HF5415.5.W47 1992   381.3'3   C92-093273-8

Cover design: Brant Cowie/ArtPlus Limited
Typesetting: Tony Gordon Ltd.
Printed and bound in Canada

Information and incidents contained in this book are based on the author's experience. Readers should use their own judgement or consult a legal expert for specific applications to their individual situations.

Stoddart Publishing gratefully acknowledges the support of the Canada Council, Ontario Arts Council and Ontario Publishing Centre in the development of writing and publishing in Canada.

CONTENTS

Introduction

Every single day, people from all walks of life suffer numerous injustices at the hands of bank tellers, insurance clerks, mechanics, retailers, teachers, and others. A silk blouse loses its color on the very first wash. A new car breaks down just minutes after leaving the showroom. An essay receives an unfair mark. Many innocent victims seethe in silence, or seek the sympathy of friends, neighbors, and relatives. Some may even complain to the offender, by phone or in person, only to encounter frustration. But few use the most effective communication tool of all — the letter.

Don't get mad . . . write!

In this age of sophisticated electronic communications, the art of writing letters has become almost obsolete. The basics of letter writing are no longer emphasized or even taught in our schools. People send memos to one another via electronic mail systems or reach for the telephone. The mighty pen has been replaced by the push button. But is the push button mightier than the pen? Not in the realm of lodging complaints. When you need to negotiate from a position of strength, when you want to maintain control of a situation, a carefully composed letter will always be immeasurably more effective.

The telephone is, of course, useful for most mundane personal and business purposes, and it does have its advantages: local calls are free, contact is usually immediate, and using it has become second nature. But consider the disadvantages: the person you wish to speak to will undoubtedly be "unavailable," or be so articulate and accomplished at fielding complaints that you will be left tongue-tied; if you do succeed in lodging your point of view, there is no written guarantee that your efforts will be rewarded; and if further action is required you will have no record of the conversation. In my experience, women are particularly ignored, both over the telephone and in person, even (especially?) by other women.

What follows will, I hope, instill in you new confidence and respect for the written word. My humorous book, *Outrageously Yours*, generously published in Canada by General Publishing in 1986, and in the U.S.A. by Putnam Publishing in 1987, illustrates the astonishing results of deliberate and blatant tongue-in-cheek correspondence. This present tome provides step-by-step instructions you can use to solve virtually any problem, however daunting. I have practiced these procedures over many years, and they have almost invariably produced the desired result, often, dare I confess, to my complete astonishment!

The primary intention of this book is to show you how to solve consumer disputes without going to court. Occasionally, however, legal action may be required, and appropriate steps for seeking restitution through small claims court are included in chapter 10. If you feel your particular circumstances warrant legal advice, the same chapter includes some pointers for selecting counsel.

1

The Basics

Most disputes result from a failure to communicate effectively. Effective communication occurs when concise information is transmitted clearly, and to the right person. Furthermore, that information must be worded so that the recipient will be receptive to it.

THE STRATEGY

Satisfactorily solving all that life tends to throw one's way requires calm and careful planning — a strategy like the one outlined below. In the following chapters we will see how this strategy can be adapted to different situations. It is essential to become familiar with the basic steps and to understand the reasons for practicing them in relevant order.

1. STAY CALM. This is essential, although it may not always be easy. Staying calm allows you to plan your approach, to maintain respect, and to stay in control. If you burst into the offending establishment at peak business hours, accuse all the staff of fraud and theft, and then threaten to burn the place down, to sue all concerned, and to set up pickets warning future customers of the conspiracy to defraud them of their life savings, a sympathetic review will not be forthcoming, and you will achieve nothing.

2. VISUALIZE YOUR OPPONENT'S REACTION. Before planning your approach, picture your opponent's reaction to your confrontation. Putting yourself in the other's shoes enables you to plan your approach.

3. ASSESS THE SITUATION. Next, you need to determine if there *really is* a problem. The best way to do this is to telephone or visit the offender. In many cases, the dispute can be resolved during this initial meeting. However, if not, and further action is required, it is important to stay calm, make careful mental or written notes of what transpires, and discover the name and status of the person you are dealing with.

Don't make more than one visit or call, because you won't have any record of what was said (although you may be grateful you don't have a record of what you said during a heated argument!). You could be wasting your time speaking to someone who does not have the authority to solve the problem. You might be dealing with a company whose employees are well versed in handling complaints: they keep you on the line while they page someone who has no intention of speaking to you anyway, pass you from colleague to colleague, take messages with the promise that someone will call you back. Waste no more time, for these people are masters of their craft and know that you will soon capitulate through sheer frustration, leaving them the winners.

If you must leave a message, leave a call-back number that will be answered during normal business hours in order to give the institution every opportunity to get in touch with you. Two days is time enough for a call to be returned.

4. DEAL WITH THE MOST SENIOR PERSON AVAILABLE. Often, of course, you can resolve a problem with the clerk or employee you dealt with originally. However, at the first sign of noncooperation, you should firmly request to talk to the most senior person with the authority to help you. If that person is not available, you should refuse to deal further with the clerk and take your leave.

5. REQUEST THE NAME OF THE PRESIDENT. Before you leave, you should request the full name of the president of the organization as well as his corporate address. This may, in some circumstances, prompt a reconsideration of your request for a refund, especially if you look determined to make use of the information.

6. CONFIRM THE INFORMATION. When you get home, confirm the name and address of the president. This is essential. Spelling anyone's name wrong does not create an endearing impression. Besides which, it makes you look amateurish, and no one is impressed by amateurs, least of all company presidents. There is no need to be nervous about verifying this information. All it takes is a simple phone call to the store or head office of the institution.

7. WRITE TO THE PRESIDENT. Why the president? There are numerous reasons:

- You will have the best chance of success. With the possible exception of the chairman, the president is the most important person in an organization and has absolute authority over everyone else in the company.

- You eliminate wasting valuable time writing to someone who is not empowered to deal with your problem.
- You give the president the opportunity of personal contact with a customer, possibly a refreshing experience!
- The president may be unaware that the company is selling faulty merchandise or providing shoddy service, which means lost customers (i.e., money), and will undoubtedly appreciate your comments, correct the problem from the top, and consequently eliminate future complaints.
- If you eventually need to file a claim in court, your case will be much stronger if you have corresponded with top management.
- By expressing your annoyance and inconvenience in writing to the president, you subtly include "damages" in your claim. A president will want to uphold the company's reputation (or if busy with more pressing matters, will simply want to get rid of you), and will probably refund all your money, even if you're not entitled to a full refund.

THE LETTER

Your letter must be carefully phrased to suit the circumstances, and it must summarize concisely the complaint and state clearly what your expectations are — a company president doesn't have the time to read your life story. Furthermore, the president will be more receptive if your tone reflects someone of equal status, someone who expects immediate action. (Another advantage of writing is that, no matter your education or background, you can communicate with anyone in the world on equal terms.)

Once you get into the habit of writing instead of getting mad, you will write with greater fluidity and confidence. After a while, you will regard presidents as no more than ordinary employees with an obligation to give you the service you deserve — which is, of course, a perfectly realistic expectation.

Never correspond by hand. *Always type any correspondence.* Even if your handwriting is excellent, it makes your letter look amateurish. Business correspondence is always typed, and you are communicating with a business person. If you do not own a typewriter or word processor, borrow one, persuade a friend to help you, or hire a professional typing or word-processing service listed in the telephone directory. (Don't forget to include this expense when you send your claim to the company.)

Your letter should be typed on good quality 8½ x 11 paper. There is no need to use letterhead, unless you have it, but your paper and envelope should look businesslike: white or a soft neutral shade best convey the message that you mean business.

Before mailing any correspondence, make a photocopy and keep it in a file along with any future correspondence as well as the bill or invoice for the goods or service, expense receipts, and any pertinent notes.

When you send your letter, make sure you address your envelope properly.

Low-Graad Manufacturing Inc.
232 Industrial Park Road
Dowtfulle, BA
H2S 2V2

For the attention of Aryu Cheep, President

PRIVATE AND CONFIDENTIAL

If the name of the addressee is placed apart from the company name, it will stand out. Putting PRIVATE AND CONFIDENTIAL on the envelope will ensure that it is opened and read by the addressee (or by the personal secretary, who will forward it in any event).

There are several ways to send your letter: by ordinary mail, registered mail, courier, or fax. Fax or mail is cheapest, and the letter will normally reach its destination. Faxed letters have an air of urgency about them that could mean more immediate action. The fax machine will record the time and date of the transmission and the fax number of the recipient. But a fax may be received by a clerk who sends it to the customer service department instead of the president, or it could be left in a pile by the machine for days, so you should always send your letter by mail, too. If you are concerned about the reliability of postal service in your area, you could send the letter by registered mail, or use a courier. I mail my letters and have not encountered any problems. (When I do, you can be sure I won't get mad — I'll write to the president of the post office!)

THE EXPENSES

Ask for receipts for all your expenses — postage, stationery, telephone calls, typing or courier services, transportation costs — and keep careful records of the amount of time you spend dealing with any problem. You will bill the offending institution for your time and expenses as part of your claim.

How much should you charge for your time? When you calculate your hourly rate, I suggest you use an hourly rate of four times your normal pay — more if your job is not well paid! You need not specify your rate on the invoice — just the total. I charge $60 an hour when I invoice "customers," and to date this has never been questioned (I type with two fingers, so my invoices are scarcely a bargain!). One of the most persuasive methods of ensuring that institutions treat their customers well is to relieve them of some money every time they fail to do so.

Now, let's put the theory into practice!

2

It's Your Money: Taking on the Banks

How often have you or someone you know been the victim of an error committed by a bank? An error can result in all kinds of headaches: an NSF check, an unexpected service charge, or a missed payment.

Banks routinely employ staff who are completely inexperienced in even the most rudimentary clerical procedures, because banks save on wages by employing unskilled help or because there is a shortage of skilled labor. Whichever the reason, it saves the banks a great deal of money at the expense and inconvenience of the customer, who is increasingly treated as a source of great irritation rather than the essential and respected reason for the banks' existence!

When an error is discovered, you can spend days trying to find someone in the branch with the intelligence to understand the nature of the error, and yet more time locating someone else who is capable of correcting it. At the end of it all, you consider yourself fortunate to have achieved a belated reversal of the mistake, a mistake that may have cost you dearly in time and reputation.

Despite the power they appear to hold over the mere mortal customer, banks are entirely responsible for their mistakes, just like any other organization or individual, and it is relatively easy to extract compensation from them. At least, it is reassuring to know that they can afford to pay for their mistakes!

INCORRECT DEBIT MEMO

Let's assume you are the owner of a house, with the inevitable mortgage to constantly remind you of your most expensive asset. Together with the monthly payment, the mortgagee relieves your bank account of the property tax portion simultaneously through the automatic payment plan, over which you have no immediate control.

Each month you deposit your paycheck, and having calculated the amount that will be debited for the mortgage and tax payment, you then plan your budget for the balance.

Last month, you received a notice from the mortgagee advising you of a minor tax adjustment — it seems they underestimated the amount required when the mortgage was renewed a year ago. The additional charge is very small, eight dollars, and you have adjusted your budget accordingly.

Unfortunately, the notification was mistyped, and your account is, in fact, being relieved of *eighty* dollars a month. You, however, are blissfully spending the money, which will no longer be available to cover your checks.

The first indication that anything is amiss arrives in your mailbox some twelve days after the mortgage payment due date. To your amazement it is a letter from the holder of your mortgage, informing you that the monthly pre-authorized check has been returned by your bank marked "Non sufficient funds," and that the check will be re-presented, together with an added collection fee of twenty dollars! Ironically, your checks issued prior to the mortgage payment date had all cleared, and the mortgagee has been hoist by his own petard, for which he is holding you responsible. Naturally, you are upset.

Now, you begin to correct matters in the most expedient manner, making careful notes of all that transpires. First of all, check the notification of increase to ensure that the mistake is definitely theirs, and that you did not misinterpret or misread the tax adjustment. Verify, too, that you haven't written any checks that have not been recorded in your register.

Once you establish that the error is unquestionably not yours, it is time to call the person who signed the letter informing you of the dishonored payment. If the letter is unsigned, ask for whoever is responsible for mortgage payment administration. Explain the circumstances carefully, and request a written explanation of why the error occurred as well as an account of what will be done to rectify the matter and compensate you for your inconvenience.

If you don't get through, and your call isn't returned after two days, it is time to write the president. (You have, of course, confirmed the spelling of his name.) You write as follows:

24 Dettor Lane
Uptite, Inutopia
F3G 2W3

The Luting Bank
1 Usurer Place
Amor, Gagee
S9C 3L1

February 22, 1992

For the attention of Watt A. Cashgrasper, President

Dear Mr. Cashgrasper,

On January 15, I received a letter from your organization referring to my mortgage, number 345234, informing me that your pre-authorized withdrawal for $978.87 had been returned NSF. I telephoned the clerk who signed the letter to gently point out that this was hardly surprising since the amount in question was some seventy-two dollars in excess of the sum notified (see enclosed copy) and allowed for in my account balance.

The clerk concerned was unable to offer an explanation, but said she would "check with her supervisor" and call back in a few minutes. To date, I have received no further communication.

Kindly forward an immediate and full explanation.

Any charges and expenses I incur as a consequence of your negligence will be invoiced to your bank for full payment.

Yours sincerely,

Broak Kliyent

Encl.

Your letter may not receive an immediate reply for numerous reasons: the president may be away on business; he may have passed the case to a subordinate, who in turn will have to contact the appropriate branch to acquire more details; there may be mail delays, and so on.

However, you are not accustomed to being kept in the dark by mere bank presidents! If you have not received a reply in, say, ten days, it is time to send a reminder to show that you mean business. Your reminder will be worded thus:

---

24 Dettor Lane
Uptite, Inutopia
F3G 2W3

The Luting Bank
1 Usurer Place
Amor, Gagee
S9C 3L1

March 5, 1992

For the attention of Watt A. Cashgrasper, President

Dear Mr. Cashgrasper,

May I expect your reply to my letter regarding my
mortgage, number 345234, of February 22, in the not
too distant future?

Yours sincerely,

Broak Kliyent

If you still haven't received a reply in a further ten days, then a letter to the chairman is in order. Such a step would, I hope, not be necessary, since the preceding letters are all that are normally required to produce results. The chairman will naturally be pleased to hear how his bank is performing in these competitive times!

24 Dettor Lane
Uptite, Inutopia
F3G 2W3

The Luting Bank
1 Usurer Place
Amor, Gagee
S9C 3L1

March 15, 1992

For the attention of Olden Welthey, Chairman

Dear Mr. Welthey,

On February 22, and again on March 5, I was obliged
to write to your president, Watt A. Cashgrasper,
concerning the appalling and unpredictable service I
am experiencing at the hands of your mortgage
department.

Thus far, Mr. Cashgrasper has not seen fit to reply to
either of my letters. Perhaps you would be good enough
to confirm that Mr. Cashgrasper has not left your employ
and whether his duties include dealing with his
correspondence.

I look forward to your earliest reply.

Yours sincerely,

Broak Kliyent

You have now sent more than enough correspondence to precipitate a thorough investigation by the highest authority, which should result in a letter of apology, and an admission of liability. If any further correspondence is called for, write to the chairman, even if you have been answered by a branch manager, vice-president, or other executive. Always mention the date and writer of previous correspondence, for example: "I have received a letter dated March

25 from your Mr. Avery Odclerk . . . ." Persist until the matter is settled to your satisfaction.

When all has been finalized, add up your expenses and prepare an invoice (don't forget to include your expenses for compiling and sending the invoice). The invoice should be sent to the president.

Broak Kliyent
24 Dettor Lane
Uptite, Inutopia
F3G 2W3

The Luting Bank
1 Usurer Place
Amor, Gagee
S9C 3L1

April 2, 1992

For the attention of Watt A. Cashgrasper, President

INVOICE

For expenses caused by mismanagement of account #345234, resulting in NSF charges, telephone calls, written correspondence, and associated costs.

Total $73.50

Terms: Payment within 14 days. Overdue accounts attract interest at 2% per month.

Within days, you should receive a check for $73.50. The bank clearly caused you financial and personal inconvenience, and your firm refusal to accommodate their negligence left them with no option but to pay up. Should they not settle, you would then send a statement, showing interest for the first month. However, as a rule, banks are usually quick at settling accounts, and it is unlikely you will need to send any reminders.

Broak Kliyent
24 Dettor Lane
Uptite, Inutopia
F3G 2W3

The Luting Bank
1 Usurer Place
Amor, Gagee
S9C 3L1

May 3, 1990

STATEMENT

Re: Account #345234

Outstanding balance dated April 2, 1992	$73.50
Interest to May 3 at 2% per month	1.47
Balance due	$74.97

A second statement, if needed, should be sent with interest compounded for the second month, giving the bank ten days to settle, failing which a court summons would be filed without further notice. Filing a small claims summons is not difficult and is described in detail in chapter 10.

FAILURE TO NOTIFY OF NSF CHECK

Let us assume you sell your old stereo system through the classified ads for $500.00. The buyer gives you a check, produces documentation verifying his address and financial standing, and leaves with the goods. Pleased with your transaction, you deposit the check into your account and rush off to purchase the latest in audio equipment.

All is well until, four weeks later, a letter from your bank arrives informing you that the $500.00 check for your old stereo has been returned NSF. Horrified, you call the purchaser only to hear a recorded voice informing you that the number is no longer in service. A quick visit confirms that the crafty purchaser has moved without leaving a forwarding address. You are, of course, upset and vow that next time you will only accept cash or certified check. However, reproaching yourself is not going to recoup the loss. If there is no hope of locating the purchaser, then a more promising avenue must be pursued.

Although, obviously, the purchaser is the cause of your dilemma, you may be able to seek damages from the bank. If there was no mail strike or other civil dispute impeding the performance of your bank, then the four weeks it took for the bank to inform you that the check had not been honored was unreasonable. But before you get carried away with glee, examine the date on the envelope containing the bank's NSF notification. If the postmark is dated three weeks prior to your receiving it, then the delay occurred in the mail and you will have no claim against the bank.

If the date is recent, however, you may have a case (remember to keep the envelope on file for proof). The amount of time banks take to clear checks depends on how sophisticated they are, on the location of the bank on which the check was issued, and on whether there were intervening weekends or holidays. But four weeks is quite unacceptable. As part of your assessment, you should verify how long it takes your bank to clear a check and send an NSF notice under normal circumstances. In my experience, it takes from eight to ten days.

You examine the debit note and its envelope, and see that there is a difference of ten days between their dates. This is all the evidence you need to stake your claim; the bank is clearly at fault.

You can, if you wish, make a telephone call to your branch to register your indignation, but frankly, I think this would be a wasted call. For the "reward" of not having to admit fault and not having to credit your account with (their) $500.00, they may be prepared to argue extensively, and you will achieve nothing. Far better is to be so outraged by this appalling lack of concern for customers' affairs, that you have no option but to contact the man at the top, and send a copy to the manager of the branch concerned.

---

65 Fairloan Avenue
Upper Province
F2R 7S2

The Bank of Magna Lucre
Lucre Towers
Goldstreets
L5G 7T3

February 5, 1992

For the attention of Franc Sterling, President

Dear Mr. Sterling,

On January 2, 1992, I deposited into my account #543 3242, Main Branch, Bank of Magna Lucre, Upper

Province, a check for $500.00. This check represented the proceeds for a used stereo system sold earlier that day to a private purchaser. On January 30, twenty-eight days after the check was deposited, I received a debit note from my branch informing me that the check had been returned unpaid.

I am unable to contact the drawer of the check, since he moved on January 22, leaving no forwarding address. Had your bank performed with the efficiency expected of an organization of your stature, as continually claimed in your comprehensive advertising, and not waited four weeks to inform me of this debit, I would have been able to collect the $500.00 from my customer. Such gross negligence is quite unacceptable. Kindly, therefore, ensure that my account is credited with the $500.00 in question, without delay.

For your interest, the debit note, dated January 18, arrived in an envelope postmarked January 28. Perhaps this meets your expectation of reasonable performance?

I look forward to your immediate reply.

Yours sincerely,

Carole M. Uzik

c.c. Manager, Main Branch, Upper Province

You may be surprised to observe that the carbon copy to your branch fails to identify the name of the manager. This is because we are dealing with the president at head office, and the status of a mere branch manager is so insignificant that his or her identity is quite unnecessary. As far as we are concerned, whether the letter reaches the manager or not is unimportant since we would not reply to any communication from that person — our response would be addressed to the president, "in reply to the letter dated ____ from your branch manager." Similarly, should you receive a phone call from the manager, the call should be acknowledged to the president, although, of course, phone calls should be avoided unless the manager is offering immediate and full capitulation. Firmly request that the caller put any message in writing.

If you have not received a reply within ten days, a sharp reminder to the chairman is in order.

---

65 Fairloan Avenue
Upper Province
F2R 7S2

The Bank of Magna Lucre
Lucre Towers
Goldstreets
L5G 7T3

February 15, 1992

For the attention of Hugh Jassets, Chairman

Dear Mr. Jassets,

On February 5, I wrote to your president, Mr. Franc Sterling, concerning the serious mismanagement of my account by your bank. To date, my concerns have yet to be addressed, or even acknowledged.

If Mr. Sterling is no longer in your employ, I should be most grateful if you could direct his successor to respond without further delay.

Yours sincerely,

Carole M. Uzik

Making sure that the chairman is keeping track of his president is always good insurance. Determined persistence on your part should result in a full credit to your account.

CREDIT CARD MAILED TO WRONG ADDRESS

When you move, you are obliged to compile long and tedious lists of friends, utilities, creditors, relatives, and so forth, who need to be informed of your new address. It is essential to notify in good time all the issuers of your credit cards of your new address, for delayed payments can have dire consequences for the card user.

Some card issuers are notorious for failing to take note of change-of-address information. Gasoline companies and department stores seem to be particularly lax in this area, so if you think a statement is overdue, call the card issuer concerned to confirm that they are aware of your new whereabouts.

Your last move is almost forgotten — you have been living in your new residence for eight months now. Life is running smoothly, and all your statements are arriving in their usual unwelcome but inevitable fashion. Approximately a month after your move, your PetroExtort gasoline card expired; you cut it up and threw it in the garbage. The company didn't bother to send you a new card, but you assumed this was because you rarely used it.

To your horror and disbelief, a letter arrives one morning from a collection agency. The tersely worded contents inform you that unless you settle the $729.55 including interest and collection fees owed to the PetroExtort Corporation, legal proceedings will commence within ten days. You call the person who signed the letter. A stern voice tells you that the account is for gasoline purchases over the past six months, and that since you failed to pay any of the statements sent, the gas company sent the file to the collection agency, who in turn just discovered your new address.

Bewildered, you tell your contact that you do not even own a credit card issued by PetroExtort, and that you certainly haven't purchased any of their products for more than a year. Predictably, the collection agent is unimpressed by your protestations. It is his job to collect the money owed, and your excuses are hardly original — he has heard innumerable variations of your theme throughout his career.

In as calm a voice as you can muster, you ask for a copy of the account to be sent to you at once, and a couple of days later the statement arrives confirming the description of the account given by the agent over the phone.

It is clear that a renewal credit card was sent to your old address and was gratefully intercepted by a keen student of personal frugality! This will have to be confirmed beyond doubt, and used to ensure that you are not held liable for the debt. Your reputation must be rescued unscathed.

Any further attempt to negotiate with the collection agency is unlikely to be productive. You must, therefore, deal directly with the PetroExtort Corporation. However, it would certainly do no harm to send a letter to the president of the agency, denying any liability whatsoever and informing him that you will be dealing with PetroExtort directly from here on. Your letter might look something like this:

---

43 Eagle Drive
Uptown
G5H 3W4

Credigrab Agencies Inc.
Skweaz Towers
Downtown
R7T 4D6

February 10, 1992

For the attention of R. U. Scrouge, President

Dear Mrs. Scrouge,

Your File #784352, which claims that I am indebted to the PetroExtort Corporation for the amount $643.78, plus interest and collection fee, for a total of $729.55, is entirely erroneous and without foundation.

I shall be ensuring that this alleged account is canceled immediately, through the offices of Mr. Costas Lotzfergas, President of PetroExtort Corporation. You will be advised of the outcome of this issue as soon as it is settled to my satisfaction. Meanwhile, I strongly advise that you refrain from further proceedings.

Yours sincerely,

Weil Phixthis

c.c. Costas Lotzfergas, President, PetroExtort Corporation

This may stay proceedings for a few days. Should the agency ignore your suggestion, and their persistence has a detrimental effect on your credit standing or causes you financial loss, then you will, of course, claim damages when the dispute is settled.

Meanwhile, you also write to the oil company as follows:

---

43 Eagle Drive
Uptown
G5H 3W4

The PetroExtort Corporation
Oil Towers
Crudetown
Y6H 2D9

February 10, 1992

For the attention of Costas Lotzfergas, President

Dear Mr. Lotzfergas,

I have received a demand from Credigrab Agencies Inc., which claims that I am indebted to your company for the amount of $643.78, plus interest, and a collection fee due to the agency, for a total of $729.55. Their reference #784352.

Since I have no business dealings with your company, I am requesting comprehensive written evidence of the premise upon which you base this totally unfounded allegation.

Please be aware that subject to the outcome of this matter, your company and its agents will be held entirely responsible for all expenses I incur as a result of your actions, including damages for my compromised credit rating.

Kindly remit by return post.

Yours sincerely,

Weil Phixthis

c.c. R. U. Scrouge, President, Credigrab Agencies Inc.

Since you are obliged to deal with two different companies, it is a good idea to send copies of your correspondence to both parties. So far, you don't know how far you may have to go in order to obtain a just conclusion. If it becomes necessary to claim costs, you may have to file a court summons against one or both parties, in which case your position will be stronger if you can demonstrate to the judge that you made every effort to keep all parties aware of your innocence from the outset.

Within a few days, you receive details of the claim, a brief explanation from the accounts department along with photocopies of twenty-seven receipts for gasoline and associated products, all charged to your account! Close inspection reveals that the card was issued shortly after you moved to your new address, and that the signatures on the receipts bear no resemblance to yours. Some even include a license plate number, again bearing no resemblance to yours. Included as well are copies of letters from PetroExtort, sent to your vacated address, demanding payment of the outstanding amount and finally informing you that the account is being handed over to a collection agency.

You now have all the information you need to see how the claim occurred, and can take appropriate steps to make sure it is quashed, without financial loss or damage to your credit standing. This requires another letter to PetroExtort.

---

43 Eagle Drive
Uptown
G5H 3W4

The PetroExtort Corporation
Oil Towers
Crudetown
Y6H 2D9

February 16, 1992

For the attention of Costas Lotzfergas, President

Dear Mr. Lotzfergas,

I am in receipt of a letter dated February 12, together with enclosures, from your Mr. Joe King, in reply to my letter of February 10.

On June 14, 1991, I informed your organization, in writing, that as of July 31, 1991, I would no longer be residing at 32 Tesco Street, Midtown, E3R 2G8, and that all future correspondence should be directed to my new address, as above.

Not only did you choose to ignore my notification, but you apparently sent a new, unsolicited credit card to my vacated address. Not surprisingly, the new card was gratefully received and used by a person unknown over a period of several months.

Since the signatures on the receipts are nothing like my own signature, and your requests for payment were not acknowledged or met, perhaps you could inform me why the receipts were not compared with my authorized signature, which I assume you still have on record. Had you taken this obvious step, and informed the police of the fraudulent use of the card, you might well have apprehended the culprit and saved us both a great deal of time and expense.

Your action has caused me considerable distress and inconvenience. I require an immediate apology, along with confirmation that I am not responsible for this account. I expect Credigrab Agencies Inc. to cease pursuing me, and any credit rating bureau to which this account may have been sent to be informed of your error.

As soon as I receive your confirmation that all the above instructions have been complied with, I shall check with all appropriate credit bureaus. You will be invoiced for my time and expenses in dealing with this matter.

Should I apply for a loan or other credit facility and be refused because my credit rating was adversely affected as a result of your negligence, be aware that I shall expect your organization to furnish me with the

loan at the same rate and terms as the declining
institution.

I anticipate your immediate reply.

Yours sincerely,

Weil Phixthis

c.c. R. U. Scrouge, President, Credigrab Agencies Inc.
(Ref:784352)

This is a strongly worded letter. Not only is it distressing to be hounded by a collection agency, but a credit rating is important, and it takes very little to destroy years of scrupulous performance. Credit bureaus have neither the desire nor the ability to investigate the individuals on their registers. Any seemingly bona fide information sent to them is filed against the relevant individual, with no check for accuracy.

You must assume that either PetroExtort or Credigrab has already filed your case with the credit bureau, and that you will have to check that the error has been corrected. You can ascertain which bureaus have you on record by phoning the loans office of a local bank. Tell the loans officer that you intend to apply for a car loan, and that since you are not sure of your rating, you wish to inspect your credit file before making the application. The officer will give you the names and addresses of the relevant bureaus, the same bureaus the banks will be using when they assess your worthiness.

Credit bureaus are happy to let individuals have access to their files. However, wait until your demands have been met in full before investigating yourself. Once you have confirmation from PetroExtort, visit the credit bureau. Take all the correspondence with you, just in case the bureau has not updated your file. Credit bureaus are entirely impartial, and will not hesitate to re-establish your rating if it is clear that you have suffered erroneously.

Remember to invoice for your expenses.

Weil Phixthis
43 Eagle Drive
Uptown
G5H 3W4

The PetroExtort Corporation
Oil Towers
Crudetown
Y6H 2D9

February 28 1992

For the attention of Costas Lotzfergas, President

<u>INVOICE #345-92</u>

For expenses incurred in contesting your erroneous claim
for damages resulting from the fraudulent use of an
unsolicited credit card by an unknown third party. Your
reference #236 784. Credigrab reference #784352.
Expenses include telephone calls, correspondence,
postage, visit to credit bureau to confirm status, etc.

Total   <u>$263.87.</u>

Terms: Net monthly

3

Up in Smoke: Your Car

From the moment you decide to "invest" in a car, you can be the victim of a host of automobile professionals, including salesmen and mechanics.

GAS OVERCHARGE ON CREDIT CARD

Since most gas stations use computerized machinery, there is virtually no margin for error, mechanical or human, in arriving at the correct price for the amount of gasoline a customer takes. Yet the gas station is probably where you are most vulnerable to a price error. Not that gasoline companies, or their employees, intentionally or routinely overcharge their customers, but you can easily pay for gas consumed by another vehicle.

Say you pull into your favorite station for a fill-up. The gas station is busy and you are in a hurry, so you hand over your credit card to the attendant, hurriedly sign the receipt, and leave. When you arrive home in the evening, you turf out your pockets and spot the gas receipt. You are shocked to discover that you have paid $43.80 for 73 liters of gas — you clearly recollect stopping the pump at $15.00 or 25 liters. Besides, your 1988 Rereenda Lorcar has a maximum tank capacity of only 30 liters!

You are naturally annoyed with yourself; you should have checked the receipt before signing it, as will be made quite clear to you if you go back to complain tomorrow. So is there any point in making a complaint? Well, probably not to the station itself. The cashier, who won't remember you anyway, will be completely powerless to rectify the matter. The owner or manager may not be able to help you, either — it may be difficult to trace the error. Besides you have a receipt you signed.

But you definitely have a case, since it was not you who initiated the error but the employee who served you. You are only responsible for failing to spot the error before you signed the receipt.

A letter to the president of the gas producer should prove fruitful. While the amount you are claiming will hardly make you a millionaire overnight, you feel it is a matter of principle. Because you can't prove your claim conclusively, it should be an appeal, rather than a demand.

---

78 Winding Avenue
Downsvale
H4J 6W2

Masev Oil Corporation
Masev Towers
Octane
B3S 8T4

February 19, 1992

For the attention of Rich Onah, President

Dear Mr. Onah,

On the morning of Sunday, February 16, I filled the gas tank of my 1988 Rereenda Lorcar, license number 254 RYH, with 25 liters of regular gasoline at 60 cents per liter, totaling $15.00. This transaction occurred at your station situated at the northwest corner of Bathover and Eastway streets, in Doversville.

The station was extremely busy at the time, and since I was trying to pay and leave as quickly as possible, in order not to delay the people waiting behind me, I did not examine my credit card receipt when it was presented for signature. To my astonishment and dismay, when I got home that evening and looked at my receipt (photocopy enclosed), I realized that I had paid for gasoline amounting to $43.80, for 73 liters. As you can see, the license number written on the receipt by the cashier matches that of my Lorcar, the tank of which has a maximum capacity of 30 liters.

I do not know whether the mistake was the result of a computer error, or whether I was mistakenly given another customer's bill. I have always received excellent service at this and all your other outlets, and I am sure the error was quite unintentional.

Under the circumstances, I would be most grateful if you could arrange to have the overcharge of $28.80 reimbursed, at your earliest convenience.

Assuring you of my continuing patronage, I thank you in anticipation.

Yours sincerely,

Frank Lee Grovling

Encl.

Since the amount claimed is very small, and you have given the impression that you are a considerate, reasonable, and above all, regular customer, there is every reason to suppose that a credit will be forthcoming. If not, however, your grounds for any legal redress are probably doubtful; although the mistake was not yours, you certainly had every opportunity to spot it. There is probably not much point in pursuing the matter further if a refund is not offered, but a letter like this is usually effective.

UNAUTHORIZED GARAGE REPAIR

There is little doubt that overcharging and needless part replacement does occur in the auto repair business. Few people know enough about their vehicle to disagree with an experienced mechanic. Even those who are knowledgeable about car maintenance are at risk because modern technology is producing a new breed of automobiles with computerized circuitry, automatic and electrically operated units, turbochargers, and so on. Even trained mechanics are baffled by the sophisticated equipment they must use to diagnose ailing vehicles. The poor owner has little hope of disputing any estimate.

It helps to learn the correct terminology — one of the best methods of defense is attack. It is unlikely you will be taken advantage of if you tell the mechanic you think the exhaust valves are not seating properly, and ask for the alternative prices for the two viable remedies — fitting a new exchange cylinder head, or grinding and possibly fitting new valves. This will gain you more respect than saying that the engine has been losing power and becoming more difficult to start over several months. Such a vague description might well trigger the installation of a complete exchange engine, at considerably greater expense than any cylinder head work.

Do some research before selecting a garage. The large chain stores, who consistently advertise specials and who guarantee absolute satisfaction, with warranties that apparently take you well into the next century, are rarely as competent and magnanimous as their reassuring TV commercials claim. The special offer is invariably a loss leader, meant to lure you onto their jack! The special price will be inflated by the cost of parts that "need" to be replaced in order to complete the job. If you insist that you just want the advertised job, you will not be given a guarantee for the work done. And of course, you will be assured that without the complete repair job, your vehicle will be a mobile death trap. As a further incentive, should you decide to take your business elsewhere, you will not be allowed to leave with your vehicle until you pay the inspection charge!

Another alternative, the repair shop of a dealership that specializes in your car make, has the advantage that the mechanics should be familiar with the intricacies of your model. However, there are disadvantages here, too. Dealerships have inflexible pricing policies — if the book rate for a repair is two hours, that is what you will pay, even if the job only takes forty-five minutes. They tend to replace complete units instead of a faulty part in the same unit, and they are more likely to replace a part than repair it. They use only genuine replacement parts made by (or for) the manufacturer of your vehicle, which may be sound policy, but can be expensive. The dealership will tell you that more economical "clone" parts are inferior.

Worth investigating are independent garages. They rely on word of mouth from satisfied customers, so the quality of their service is usually excellent. Their labor rates may be flexible, and since they don't have to buy their parts from one source, they are probably able to supply cheaper parts. A local resident who uses a particular garage should be able to advise you about their reliability and integrity.

Whichever you choose, it's worth doing a little investigation. An ounce of prevention is worth a ton of cure in the car repair business.

Assume you are on your way to an important meeting when your car develops an acute problem, and you just make it to a nearby garage. The owner of the garage tells you that it sounds like the carburetor is suffering from fuel starvation, and that if you sign the work authorization, he will check it out later in the morning and call you with the diagnosis and estimate. You have no alternative, so you leave your car, catch a cab, and head off to your meeting, hoping that whatever is wrong can be repaired quickly and inexpensively.

Despite the inauspicious start to the morning, your meeting is short and you arrive at your office just before eleven. There is no message for you from the garage, so you immediately call them. The owner tells you that the fuel pump is badly corroded and only works intermittently. The price for a new

26

pump, including labor, will be approximately $280.00. He promises to have it ready for you by six o'clock. You give him the go-ahead.

Just before six, you arrive at the garage, full of anticipation at the prospect of being reunited with your faithful conveyance, brought back to unaccustomed youthful performance for the not unreasonable sum of $280.00. Your initial joy disappears when you are presented with a bill for $734.65, which is somewhat in excess of the amount agreed to over the telephone!

In deep shock, you examine the bill and discover that the price for fitting the fuel pump has mysteriously increased to $295.00. Furthermore, your car has been fitted with an exchange carburetor, for an additional surprise of $439.65! Immediately, you question the garage owner about the increase in price for the pump, and the reason for changing the carburetor without prior notification and agreement. He offers a reasonable explanation for the additional cost of the pump. The carburetor, however, is a different matter. You were given a definite and binding estimate for installing a pump, with no indication that anything further would be required. The owner explains that even with the new pump, the car's performance did not improve. The mechanic made some adjustments to the carburetor, but it, too, was in such bad shape that it needed replacing.

You argue, quite rightly, that since the garage did not have your authority to do the additional work, you are not responsible for paying for it. By now, the owner is less than sympathetic to your reaction. He tells you that unless the bill is paid in full, the car will not be permitted to leave the premises.

In any dispute over a bill, it is to your advantage to pay the amount claimed, to prove both that you are acting in good faith and that you are solvent. You can indicate that you do not agree to your liability by writing "paid under protest" on the invoice, check, or credit card receipt.

You reluctantly agree to pay. But how should you pay? You could use a check and then call your bank first thing in the morning to put a stop payment on it. This would give you better negotiating power, but although it is unlikely you would be convicted, this is fraudulent behavior and would not enhance your credibility should you have to go to court. The garage could argue that the reason you disputed the amount was that you didn't have sufficient funds to cover the necessary work, and the stopped check tends to confirm these suspicions. Also, if you stop payment on the check, the garage will probably initiate proceedings against you, which will damage your credit rating and create a negative impression on a judge.

Meanwhile back at the garage, you have decided to pay by credit card. You have little choice, since the garage predictably enough has refused your check. You write "paid under protest" on the receipt, then you depart in your refurbished conveyance. Later that evening, with your car safely parked at home, you plan your campaign to recover the amount overcharged.

According to the huge sign in the forecourt, the garage sells gas produced by Supafume Petroleum. However, the invoice reveals that the garage bears the name A. V. Ridge Wrench Auto. Supafume may not be legally liable for the actions of A. V. Ridge Wrench Auto, but it will be concerned about damages to its hard-earned reputation and may put pressure on the garage owner to refund your money or make good itself. You will more likely receive a concerned and responsible reaction from a large corporation than from an independent garage, even if it is not directly responsible for the actions of the garage. The gas company stands to make a great deal of money from you during your motoring life expectancy — they won't want to lose you as a customer. Therefore, you write the president of Supafume Petroleum.

---

76 Drive Avenue
Lower Ridges
K4W 7Z9

Supafume Petroleum Inc
1 Octane Boulevard
Welltown
T3H 3Q8

February 20, 1992

For the attention of Hy Pumprise, President

Dear Mr. Pumprise,

On the morning of February 18, my 1986 Tarmak Shredar De Luxe was suddenly afflicted by a serious misfire as I was driving to my office. Since the car appeared to be on the brink of stalling, I was obliged to take it to the nearest garage.

Fortunately, or so I thought, the nearest garage was the Supafume Petroleum station at 534 Kamuter Street, Upper Ridges. I left my car with Mr. Ridge, the owner, who promised to call me at my office as soon as he had diagnosed the problem. When I arrived at my office at eleven o'clock, there was no message from Mr. Ridge, so I called him immediately. He informed me that the car needed a new fuel pump, which would be installed by the end of the day for a total price of $280.00.

Confident that a garage run by an organization of your reputation could be relied upon to perform a fair and workmanlike job, I authorized him to complete the work, and looked forward to collecting my car at the end of the day.

My confidence, however, was shattered by the size of the bill that greeted my arrival at the garage. Somehow, the $280.00 quote had grown to an astonishing $734.65! The $280.00 estimate for the fuel pump had increased to $295.00, which was reasonable. Mr. Ridge's explanation for the additional $439.65 was, however, unacceptable. I was told that this was for an exchange carburetor, which was installed entirely without my knowledge or authority. The garage made no attempt to gain my authorization for the replacement carburetor.

It is odd that both the fuel pump and the carburetor should fail simultaneously, since these two parts function independently of each other. However, the work has now been completed, and I am hardly in a position to verify the necessity of such an unexpected undertaking. The point remains that since I did not authorize the caburetor installation and was not given the option to refuse the extra work, I was certainly not prepared to pay the increased amount on the bill. Not surprisingly, I was not allowed to leave with my car until the full amount had been settled, which left me with no choice but to pay up, despite my protests.

I am frankly appalled at this treatment, particularly since the Supafume impeccable reputation has always been upheld in my past experiences with your retail outlets. I would therefore be most grateful to receive your confirmation that this incident is not one that you are prepared to accept and that a refund of my $439.65 can be anticipated in the very near future.

I enclose for your information a photocopy of the invoice and credit card receipt for the job in question. I look forward to hearing from you.

Yours sincerely,

Mustapha Nubike

Encl.

c.c. Axel V. Ridge, A. V. Ridge Wrench Auto

This letter should inspire the president to investigate your complaint without delay, and you should be sent a reply confirming this.

Your letter has made it clear that you have a valid grievance, yet you have made no threats of legal recrimination, or forcefully demanded a refund. Instead you have given Supafume the opportunity to maintain their unblemished reputation and to retain you as a customer. You have made it clear that this is a matter of principle between two reputable parties, you and Supafume, and that you expect the refund just as soon as they have verified your claim.

If Supafume refuses to help you, then you will have to confront Mr. Ridge's emporium directly. This could be a formidable challenge; you have discovered to your cost that A. V. Ridge is less than understanding. Since you have already dealt with the owner, there is no one with greater authority to turn to. Nonetheless, it is not yet time to capitulate.

First, do a little research into the repair associations, motoring clubs, or similar organizations the garage claims to be affiliated with. The invoice and any notices inside or outside the garage may give you some clues, and your local library will be able to give you the names and addresses of consumer and business directories and guides in which the garage might be recommended. Compile a list of all these organizations, along with the name and title of whoever is in charge of them, and send them all copies of the letter you are now going to send Mr. Ridge.

Remember to send a copy of the letter to Supafume Petroleum. Never give up! Just because they claim they are not liable for any repair problems does not mean that you cannot continue to pressure them. They may still use their influence if you prove to be a serious nuisance!

If the garage was an independent, with no gasoline outlet, this is also the letter you would have sent to the proprietor as your first step.

76 Drive Avenue
Lower Ridges
K4W 7Z9

A. V. Ridge Wrench Auto
534 Kamuter Street
Upper Ridges
W6E 2G4

February 25, 1992

For the attention of Axel V. Ridge, Proprietor

Dear Mr. Ridge,

On the morning of February 18, I brought my 1986 Tarmak Shredar De Luxe to your garage for attention to a misfire that had developed as I drove to work.

You explained that you could not immediately diagnose the problem, but you would examine the car later and call me at my office with your verdict. Meanwhile, you insisted that I sign a blank work order, without which you said you had no authority to do any work on the car. Trusting that this was a mere formality, and since I had no alternative, I complied with your instructions and departed.

When I arrived at my office at eleven, there was no message from you, so I called you. You told me that my car needed a new fuel pump, which you could install by the end of the day for the inclusive price of $280.00. I gave you the authority to go ahead with the work.

When I arrived to pick up my vehicle, I was presented with a bill for $734.65, comprising $295.00 for the fuel pump and an additional $439.65 for a new carburetor, which was installed without my consent. I was quite prepared to pay the additional $15.00 for the fuel pump, since I accept that no estimate can be completely accurate, but I question the need for the new carburetor. I find it a remarkable coincidence that both the pump and carburetor failed simultaneously, since they work independently of each other.

31

You made no attempt to inform me of your decision to install the carburetor, despite my being at my telephone all day. You refused to discuss my concerns about this huge increase over your original agreed quotation, and told me that unless I paid in full, you would keep my car until the account was settled. Having no choice, I paid your account in full, under protest, and left with my car.

The fact remains, however, that you installed a carburetor without my knowledge or permission. Therefore, I require that my bill be reduced accordingly, and that you remit to me the sum of $439.65.

I expect to receive your check without delay.

Yours sincerely,

Mustapha Nubike

c.c. Ryder Totruc, President, Automobile Association
     May I. Chekyew, President, Better Business Bureau
     Ruth Less, President, Auto Repair Dealers Association
     Hy Pumprise, President, Supafume Petroleum Inc.

A small business does not make as much profit as a large one, and may therefore be less willing, or able, to afford to give refunds. To win this one, you will need to be very determined and tenacious.

By sending the owner a letter that shows you have done your research and sent copies to organizations that might have some influence over him, or with whom he would like his reputation to remain unblemished, you show him that he must take you seriously. Although you are unlikely to receive any written response, there is a good chance that he may call you to discuss a partial refund. The golden rule of not negotiating over the phone and insisting on written confirmation of any verbal promise may have to be broken in a case like this. Most small garages' expertise in correspondence is limited to handwritten estimates, signing for delivered parts, and writing up invoices. You will probably have to discuss the matter over the phone or at the garage. The phone is probably the safer option, if you want to avoid unhelpful pressure from the mechanics in attendance.

It is up to you whether to accept a partial refund. Keep in mind that your car has benefited from the new carburetor, despite your reluctance to pay for it. Had the garage called you and quoted you an additional $220.00 (half the amount you were charged) for a carburetor, you might have given them the authority to go ahead. And if you go to court, and the garage proves that a new carburetor was needed and that the failure to notify you of this prior to installing it was just an unintentional oversight, the judge may well decide that a fifty-fifty liability is appropriate.

Should you feel strongly that you will not settle for anything less than a full refund, then you will have to convince the garage owner that you are determined to do whatever is necessary to get your money back. You now visit your local small claims court to pick up some claim forms, which are usually free. The only difficult part of this procedure is discovering the address of the court. It is usually buried in the government section of your telephone directory. If you cannot find it, directory assistance or the local library should be able to help.

At this stage, you are not going to file a claim, but you complete the form with the intention of filing if necessary. Whether you actually intend to take the matter to court is irrelevant at the moment. The object is to convince the garage that you do. To this end you must fill out the form with the details of the claim. (For more information about small claims court and the form, see chapter 10.) Make a photocopy to send with your letter.

You can now write your final letter to the garage, enclosing a copy of the claim form, which will carry a lot more weight than promises of legal action.

---

76 Drive Avenue
Lower Ridges
K4W 7Z9

A. V. Ridge Wrench Auto
534 Kamuter Street
Upper Ridges
W6E 2G4

March 20, 1992

For the attention of Axel V. Ridge, Proprietor

Dear Mr. Ridge,

Further to my claim for a refund of $439.65 charged by your garage on February 18, 1992, for the installation of a carburetor, without my knowledge or authorization, to my 1986 Tarmak Shredar De Luxe, as detailed in my letter of February 25.

To date I have received no acknowledgment or offer in reply to my claim, and unless this amount is refunded in full by Wednesday, April 3, 1992, a summons will be filed with the court without further notice.

Prior to filing the claim, I enclose a copy for your information.

Yours sincerely,

Mustapha Nubike

Encl.

c.c. Ryder Totruc, President, Automobile Association
     May I. Chekyew, President, Better Business Bureau
     Loen Knogud, Director, Upper Ridges Credit Bureau
     Ruth Less, President, Auto Repair Dealers Association
     Hy Pumprise, President, Supafume Petroleum Inc.

Copies of the letter should be sent to the associations listed in your letter, including the credit bureau, in order to further bring about a change of heart in Axel Ridge. Do not, however, include copies of the summons with the copy letters; send only the one to the garage. You have given notice that the claim will not be filed until April 3; your circulating copies of the claim prematurely to parties who are not directly involved in the dispute could be interpreted as prejudice by your unreasonable anticipation of a negative response to your letter before the expiry of the advised deadline.

It is hoped that this final demand will convince Mr. Ridge that to contest the matter further is not in his interest, and you will receive your refund within a couple of weeks. In any case, you will have exercised all the options available for settling the claim without resorting to court proceedings, and if you are out of luck, you can at least be satisfied that you did your best, or you can file the claim in court as promised.

FAULTY REPAIR JOB

It is wise to confirm the duration and extent of a guarantee for parts and labor before you give permission for any work to be done on your car. This is usually not done because you just want to know how much the repair will cost and when the car will be ready. Once the job is completed, you assume the repaired part will outlast the car, or last a reasonable time. Few garages give a separate guarantee, in addition to their normal invoice.

If you look at the back of the invoice, you may find a blanket warranty covering everything for a brief period of time or an equally unrealistic number of miles, "whichever occurs first," and a disclaimer denying liability for secondary or consequential damages resulting from failure of the new parts or defective workmanship. The period is often expressed in days rather than months. Ninety days appears more reassuring than three months.

The mileage guarantee may be misleading. A 10,000 kilometer (6,000 mile) guarantee could expire after 60 days if you drive 150 kilometers (90 miles) a day. Some garages offer more realistic warranties, up to a year, or 20,000 kilometers, which might appear reasonable, but in reality may be far from what should be expected.

For example, if you bought a new engine that failed at 21,000 kilometers (13,000 miles), and the garage denied any liability because the warranty had expired, this would clearly be way below reasonable expectation for such a considerable outlay. The life expectancy of a car engine nowadays is more than 200,000 kilometers (125,000 miles).

Even when a repair fails within the warranty period, you may be presented with a hefty bill for labor, since "parts only" is a frequently used clause. If a failed repair is put right by the garage responsible, and you are then given a bill for labor, you must refuse to accept liability for this arbitrary distinction. You have paid in good faith for a job that must have a reasonable life expectancy. If it does not meet these expectations, then the seller must do whatever is required to make good, entirely at his expense. There is no logic, and no legislation, that draws a line between materials and labor, yet garages collectively and individually practice this policy.

Suppose you paid $2,000.00 for extensive dental treatment, which had to be repeated three months later because of faulty workmanship. The dentist's labor cost could be as much as 90% of the total. But if you were presented with a bill for $1,800.00, since only the parts were covered, I daresay your reaction would be less than sympathetic, and you would fight the charge tooth and nail.

Garages cannot, legally or morally, decide on their own terms of liability to suit their individual business principles. The usual disclaimer in the warranty that absolves the garage from any liability arising from secondary or consequential damage resulting from defective parts or workmanship is deliberately intended to dissuade the customer from taking advantage of his legal entitlements.

If, for example, you have a new set of tires installed, and a couple of hours later one of your front wheels falls off because the mechanic forgot to tighten the wheel nuts, then the garage is entirely responsible for any and all claims that arise from the incident. Whatever the printed terms and conditions, they are entirely irrelevant, even if your signature shows your agreement with the terms. The garage might be able to mitigate a small reduction in the extent of their liability in extreme cases — for example, if it could prove that you were an expert mechanic and that, therefore, you should have realized the wheel was loose and stopped before it came off.

Consumer protection legislation is comprehensive in many countries, including Canada and the U.S., and individuals and businesses cannot tailor terms to their particular ideals and expect customers to reduce their expectations accordingly.

Say the alternator on your 1988 Carnidge Extreme died seven months ago and was replaced for $325.23 at a local garage. At the time of the repair, you were told that you would also need a new voltage regulator because a malfunction of the alternator usually causes invisible damage to the regulator. Knowing that electricity can work in strange ways, you agree to both repairs.

Then, while driving home from work one day, you notice the ignition warning light is on, and pull over to investigate. A careful inspection under the hood reveals that nothing is obviously wrong, but the light refuses to go out. Clearly something is not right, and you decide to drive to the garage that installed the new alternator seven months ago.

Fortunately, the car makes it there. You describe the problem to the mechanic, explaining that the symptoms are the same as those that prompted the installion of a new alternator a few months back, and that you can scarcely believe that it has lasted for so short a time. The mechanic tells you to leave the car, which will be attended to first thing in the morning, and you catch a bus home, hoping for a quick and inexpensive solution. Before leaving, you note the reading on the odometer so that you can check how far you have traveled since the last repair, and it reads 53,674 kilometers (approx. 30,000 miles).

When you get home, you are relieved to discover that you still have the receipt for the original repair, and that the odometer reading at the time was 41,432 kilometers (approx. 25,000 miles). Grumbling that 12,000 kilometers (7,500 miles) of life is somewhat less than you were hoping for from the new parts, you turn to the back of the invoice to read the warranty. Less than reassuring, it states that the workmanship and parts installed are guaranteed for 26 weeks, or 10,000 kilometers (6,000 miles), whichever occurs first. Needless to say, if it is necessary to produce the invoice in order to qualify for a free replacement, the service manager will be quick to point out that the warranty has expired, and that the garage is no longer responsible.

The next morning, feeling somewhat apprehensive, you call the garage and are told that the alternator is beyond repair and that it must be replaced.

There is no point in discussing the warranty at this stage, since the work will have to be done in any case, and it is in your interest to have it done as soon as possible. You therefore give the garage authority to go ahead, and do a little research in anticipation of any dispute that might ensue later. At least your car will be repaired and ready to go, no matter what transpires when you pick it up.

Assuming the worst, that the garage will indeed adhere rigidly to the conditions of its warranty, you should now call two or three reputable repair shops in order to be able to present their guarantee conditions for comparison if need be. Call a dealer (A) who specializes in your make of car, a garage (B) that does only auto-electrical repairs, and a large national garage chain (C). Ask them how much they charge for the same job, the length and type of their warranty, and also how long, in their professional opinion and experience, such a repair should be expected to last, notwithstanding any guarantee. Make careful notes of their answers. If necessary during your later negotiations, use only the answers that exceed your own expired warranty terms. Say, for example, A quotes a price of $368.00, with a warranty of 12 months or 20,000 kilometers, B charges $297.00 with a guarantee of 12 months or 18,000 kilometers, and C wants $342.00 with a warranty of 12 months or 20,000 kilometers. And all three assure you that a new alternator should last for at least 50,000 kilometers.

Now you go to collect your car, taking your original invoice with you. The proprietor greets you with the job sheet covering your repair, but before he begins any calculations, you produce your bill and suggest firmly that since the original repair failed well before expectation and since he will be sending the part back to the supplier for compensation, you do not expect to be charged for the job. Predictably, he examines the proffered bill in order to assess his liability. After a brief trip to confirm the reading on the odometer, he informs you that the warranty has expired, and that you will have to pay for the job in full.

This is where you introduce the terms under which his competitors do business. Don't arouse hostility by suggesting that his terms are deliberately set below acceptable levels, but name and quote the three installers you spoke to, and inform him that they all volunteered that you should have had 50,000 trouble-free kilometers from a new alternator. Point out that at the time of the original repair, you had no idea what the warranty comprised as you had not looked at the back of the invoice, and had naturally assumed that your repair should have lasted much longer.

Assure him that you have great faith in his ability and reputation, and because you assume that his workmanship and the quality of his parts are at least as good as those of his competitors, you find it strange that they offer better terms of satisfaction than his. Remind him that you prefer to use his garage for whatever reason you think is most appropriate and convincing. Perhaps he was recommended to you (name the person who made the recommendation if you can), or you and your family have always had excellent service in the past, or you know you can always rely on a smaller garage like his for personal and reliable attention. By appealing to his conscience, you hope that he will demonstrate he is willing and able to match the terms of his competitors.

Of course, you acknowledge that he is entirely blameless for the part failure, since he did not make the alternator and was just the unlucky recipient of a defective part. Cajoling him into the position of having to protect his reputation will be more productive than provoking an argument by casting doubts on his ability or integrity.

Your verbal strategy will be particularly effective if the discussion is held within earshot of employees or other customers. By matching his competitors' guarantees, he will demonstrate his confidence in the performance of his garage. He would not want it understood that his questionable standard of service dictates a restricted warranty! If he stands his ground, then you will have to take steps similar to those described in the previous section.

Resist the temptation to turn the discussion into a vigorous argument, even if all your persuasive tactics fail. Instead pay the bill, remembering to mark the invoice and credit card receipt "paid under protest," and remove your car from the premises. If the garage is owned by, or conspicuously markets the products of, a major oil company, then write to the president as follows:

---

56 Rectory Lane
Higher Meadows
Y5M 2D1

Liquid Petroleum Corporation
Liquid Center
Burnetown
F5G 3E6

March 2, 1992

For the attention of Lou Nattic, President

Dear Mr. Nattic,

On July 25, 1991, I took my 1988 Carnidge Extreme
to your garage located at 1563 Green Street, Middle

Meadows, to have a failed electrical system diagnosed and corrected. I was informed that I needed a new alternator, and was advised that the voltage regulator should be replaced at the same time because it would probably have been damaged by the failure of the alternator.

I agreed to have the work done, and paid the invoice for $325.23 on the understanding that I could now anticipate an extensive period of trouble-free driving. My expectation was short-lived, however, when after a mere 12,000 kilometers (7,500 miles), the new alternator failed completely on February 26, and I was obliged to go back to your garage so that the repair could be made a second time.

To make matters worse, the proprietor, Mr. A. Paul Ling, refused to replace the faulty parts under warranty, and pointed out that the terms under which he operates limit the longevity of his workmanship to 10,000 kilometers (6,000 miles), as stated inconspicuously on the back of his invoice. I informed Mr. Ling that I had checked with three of his competitors and that they all had warranties for 1 year and/or 20,000 kilometers (12,000 miles), but he was unimpressed and insisted that I pay for the job again or he would keep my car until the account was settled. Having no choice in the matter, I paid the $325.23 under protest, and removed my car from the premises.

I am shocked to find that an organization of your reputation treats its regular customers with such minimal consideration, and I enclose copies of both invoices for your immediate attention.

Please let me know at your earliest convenience that you will be making a complete refund of the bill, dated March 1, 1992, and that a warranty more appropriate to the standards one might expect from the Liquid Petroleum

Corporation will be instigated by all your facilities
without delay.

Yours sincerely,

Ray Vingmad

Encls.

c.c. A. Paul Ling. Porfix Garage Ltd

If the garage is controlled or owned by Liquid Petroleum, your letter should produce results. If, however, Liquid Petroleum disclaims any liability on the grounds that Mr. Ling is the president of Porfix Garage Ltd., which is in no way connected to Liquid Petroleum other than as a retailer of their gasoline and associated products, then, as in the preceding chapter, you will have to address the garage directly, as follows:

---

56 Rectory Lane
Higher Meadows
Y5M 2D1

Porfix Garage
1563 Green Street
Middle Meadows
Y4X 7N8

March 9, 1992

For the attention of A. Paul Ling, President

Dear Mr. Ling,

You will recall that on February 26, 1992, I brought my
1988 Carnidge Extreme to your garage because a
warning light was on, indicating that the electrical
system had failed.

Since you had recently checked the system and installed
a new alternator and voltage regulator, I brought the car
to you again since it was possible that one of the new
parts might need some minor adjustment. To my
complete surprise, you told me that the alternator, newly

installed 12,000 kilometers ago, had burnt out and that it would have to be replaced again, together with the regulator. Naturally I had no choice but to agree to the replacement, but I assumed that since the original repair had lasted for such a short time, I would not be held responsible for further expense.

However, you presented me with another bill for $325.23, along with the explanation that the back of your original invoice described a warranty of only 10,000 kilometers. I voiced my opinion that this warranty had not been made clear to me at the time of the repair and that it was well below that expected from a garage with any confidence in the quality of its workmanship. I pointed out that three of your competitors back up their work with warranties for 1 year or 20,000 kilometers.

Nevertheless, you refused to negotiate, and I was obliged to pay you the full amount, under protest, in order to secure the release of my vehicle. Please be aware that I am convinced that your warranty is in no way appropriate to the repair in question, and that it is inferior to those given by your competitors. Furthermore, your warranty does not comply with the standards established by current consumer protection legislation.

Therefore I insist that my $325.23 be refunded at once and that your garage issue me a more comprehensive guarantee covering the work that was required after the premature failure of the first repair. Please be aware that I am prepared to take whatever steps are necessary to ensure that my money is refunded in full.

Yours sincerely,

Ray Vingmad

c.c. Lou Nattic, President, Liquid Petroleum Corporation
Ryder Totruc, President, Automobile Association
Ruth Less, President, Auto Repair Dealers Association
May I. Chekyew, President, Better Business Bureau

Again, you have done your homework, finding out the names of businesses or associations that might be unhappy to learn that their trading principles are under heavy attack, and you have sent their presidents copies of the letter. You could also send a copy to the head of the relevant consumer affairs department, state, provincial, or federal, that has jurisdiction over Mr. Ling's particular business. The government section in your local telephone directory will supply this, or your library should be able to help.

As I have described in the preceding section of this chapter, you may be offered a partial refund over the telephone. If that does not meet with your requirements, then a final letter will have to be sent, again with a photocopy of a court summons, to show that you really do mean business.

---

56 Rectory Lane
Higher Meadows
Y5M 2D1

Porfix Garage Ltd.
1563 Green Street
Middle Meadows
Y4X 7N8

March 30, 1992

For the attention of A. Paul Ling, President

Dear Mr. Ling,

I refer to my letter of March 9, 1992, requiring a refund of the $325.23 paid to your garage under protest on February 27, 1992, for the installation of an alternator and voltage regulator, replacing the units installed 12,000 kilometers previously and not covered by adequate or notified warranty.

Since you have not responded to my letter or settled my claim, please be aware that unless full payment is received by Monday, April 13, 1992, a court summons will be filed without further notice.

I enclose for your information a copy of the claim.

Yours sincerely,

Ray Vingmad

Encl.

c.c. Lou Nattic, President, Liquid Petroleum Corporation
     Ryder Totruc, President, Automobile Association
     Ruth Less, President, Auto Repair Dealers Association
     May I. Chekyew, President, Better Business Bureau
     Len Dasent, Director, Greater Meadows Credit Bureau

This should be more than enough to convince your opponent that he must take immediate action in order to protect his reputation and credit rating, and to forestall the summons. Unless he is convinced that your claim is unreasonable, a quick response can be anticipated. Again, if he offers a compromise payment, you will have to decide whether to accept. If you feel you must adhere to your principles and be paid in full, you can file the summons as described in chapter 10.

USED CAR FAILS SAFETY STANDARDS

Nothing presents a greater challenge than finding a used car that is in good condition and suits your budget. Besides the bewildering variety of makes, models, and vintages, there are inexplicable differences in asking prices.

Logic would dictate that the higher the price, the better the quality, and that a car in exceptional condition will command a higher price than a particularly tired model of the same year. However, most sellers exaggerate the condition of the vehicle on offer and consequently inflate the price to match the described condition. The asking price is, therefore, not necessarily a reliable guide to the condition of a vehicle.

Before you embark on your search, you should ascertain the real market value of your intended purchase. There are monthly trade guides that list the wholesale and retail prices of virtually all makes and vintages available, and you should have this information before you start bargaining in earnest. Although these guides are only available to the trade, your bank will have a copy so that its loans officer can calculate how much to lend you should you need financing. Call the loans officer, tell her that you will require financing for the purchase of your preferred make and vintage, and she will tell you what that model is currently worth.

You will find all types of advertisers in your search: large retailers, who are usually dealers for a particular make; much smaller "back-street" dealers, who offer a variety of different makes; and private individuals.

A reputable large dealer may appear to be the most reliable of the alternatives. If he is backed by one of the larger manufacturers, he will be mindful of their need to protect their reputation, and his performance will be geared accordingly. He will, presumably, be supported by the manufacturer he represents, a fact in your favor should you need to return a car for a subsequent repair. He will probably sell only recent models in good condition to protect his image. However, there are some disadvantages to buying from a large dealer: you will be restricted to the models he carries, since other makes taken as trade-ins may be sold via the wholesale market to other dealers; his prices are likely to be high; and bargaining for a discount may be a challenge, if he is in good shape financially and therefore in no hurry to sell. On balance, however, the big dealer is probably a good choice.

Should you not find what you want from a dealership, you might try the numerous back-street dealers, who usually have an extensive range of models, vintages, and prices. Their overheads are lower than those of a large outlet, which is usually reflected in their prices, and they are invariably keen to make a sale, and will haggle for hours if they smell a positive outcome. This means that you can often bring down the price by a surprisingly large amount if you are unmoved by the dealer's pleas of poverty. There are possible drawbacks to keep in mind, too. In most cases, the smaller dealer has little knowledge of the history or condition of the vehicle up for sale; it was probably bought at auction, after little more than a brief inspection and a glance at the mileage, or bought from another dealer who felt it represented a risk. Often, a dealer does nothing but put the price on the windshield, and only takes a closer look at the vehicle if a sale is conditional on an inspection.

Repairs are not always a dealer's business, and if the car you buy needs attention in order to pass safety inspection, the dealer may require you to pay for the necessary repairs unless they are minor. Of course, you may be fortunate enough to end up with a good car at a good price.

Another alternative is to buy from a private seller. You have the advantage of dealing with the owner rather than an agent. The owner best knows the reliability and general performance of his car, but you will have to decide whether the seller is honest. A test drive with an owner can reveal how the car has been treated. If the owner crunches the gears, screeches around corners, and constantly slams on the brakes you can safely deduce that the car has probably not enjoyed conditions conducive to a long life expectancy! With private sellers you can probably negotiate a considerable reduction in price: they are usually keen to make a quick sale, since selling through newspapers can be a trying business. So if you make a reasonable offer and produce a convincing wad of cash, you might have yourself a deal.

Make a deposit sufficient to show that you are serious, but don't pay the full price for the car and drive off with it at this point. You will need to conduct a lien search through your local transportation ministry (check the government section of your telephone directory) before returning with the balance. This will tell you whether the car is paid for, or if not, how much of it is still owned by the bank or other lender, or whether a garage has a lien against an unpaid service or repair account. There is a nominal fee of around five dollars for this search, and you must have the vehicle's serial number, and the name and address of the owner. A lien search is money well spent, since it can save considerable expense later on. If there is a lien on the vehicle, then you must make sure that it is discharged with documentary proof before proceeding with the purchase, or make arrangements to reduce the amount you pay for the car accordingly.

If you buy a vehicle from a seller who assures you that the title is clear, and you subsequently discover that this is not the case, you can of course claim the amount in question back, but this can be time consuming and inconvenient, and if you do not have enough money to clear the lien, you may lose the vehicle to the lien holder until the account is settled. If you buy from a dealer, a lien search shouldn't be necessary, since a dealer should have done a search before acquiring the vehicle.

No matter where you buy your car, the seller is obliged to provide you with a vehicle that conforms to the description of its condition, whether verbal or written, and the seller must also ensure that it is suitable for the purpose for which it is intended, which means that it must be safe and roadworthy.

You may find both private sellers and dealers who will sell you a car that has not passed a government safety inspection. In order to protect themselves they will give you a receipt bearing the legend "uncertified — as is." A car may be legitimately sold with both parties aware it is uncertified, but this does not absolve the seller from liability if the car subsequently fails the safety inspection. If a car does not pass the inspection, then it cannot be used for the purpose for which it is intended, and unless the buyer was informed of the extent and cost of the repairs needed to make the car roadworthy, and agreed to the purchase in full realization that money would have to be spent before it could be used on the road, then the seller is liable for the amount required to ensure certification.

The disclaimer "as is," used to protect sellers from the repercussions of their negligence, is vague and meaningless. The phrase cannot be legally interpreted to indicate that a product is substandard or dangerous. Vendors who sell vehicles that will not, or may not, pass a safety inspection should state clearly on the receipt, for signature by both parties, that the vehicle is unsuitable for use on the public roads because it has not passed a safety inspection, and is therefore sold strictly as parts and not as a complete vehicle — or words to that effect. And the vehicle should be rendered inoperable.

Therefore, if you have purchased a car that has failed to live up to the glowing terms in which it was described, or has been pronounced to be in dangerous condition by the police or a garage, all is not lost! Enlightened legal opinion is rapidly and correctly abandoning the caveat, "Let the buyer beware," and in the case of used cars, owners or dealers are presumed to know the condition of the vehicles they are selling and must disclose any faults, whether or not they are visibly apparent, to any potential purchasers. If they fail to do so, you can claim damages, which is the amount required to bring the vehicle up to legal roadworthiness and any other described condition that it does not meet. Or you can return the vehicle for a full refund, and cancel the contract of sale.

Let us assume that you have found the car you are looking for at a small back-street dealer who assures you that it is in excellent condition. After much haggling, you agree on a price, but when you request that the car be certified, the dealer protests that since he let you have the car for such a generous discount, the cost of certification and any work necessary to bring it up to standard will have to be added to the purchase price. He pleads that any further expense, no matter how small, will mean a loss for him, and that since the car is obviously in good shape, you will easily be able to get it certified yourself. Thus, swayed by your outstanding ability to outwit a professional car dealer at the negotiating game, and by sympathy for the unfortunate dealer, who seems like such a nice fellow, you agree to buy the car uncertified. The dealer takes your money, gives you a receipt marked "No warranty or safety certificate — as is," together with the necessary ownership papers, and shakes your hand exuberantly while assuring you that the car will be no trouble at all. You drive your new machine happily off his lot and head for your local garage, which you have used for years and know to be honest and competent, to have the car certified.

Your mechanic is uncharacteristically quiet when you tell him how much you paid for the car, and tells you he will call you later in the day after he has given it a thorough inspection. Confident, you leave it with him, and go home to await the hour when you can collect your freshly certified acquisition. When the phone rings at the end of the afternoon, you are somewhat surprised to learn that your mechanic wants you to drop by "to go over a few problems."

You head straight to the garage, where you are introduced to the underside of your car, which is elevated for inspection. In shocked disbelief, you listen to a comprehensive list of serious faults: the chassis is badly rusted and requires extensive welding and new floor panels; two tires need to be replaced; the muffler is leaking where it has been temporarily repaired with tape and putty; two ball joints on the front suspension are worn out; and both springs in the rear suspension are broken. Otherwise, the car is fine!

Correcting these problems will cost $1,280.00, and the work will take four days to complete. There is some good news, however: the rest of the car is in good order, and when the repairs are done, you will be the owner of a car that meets your original expectation. These words of comfort do little to restore your faith in human nature. You only paid $3,200.00 for the car, and for this together with the repair bill you could have bought a newer model.

You will now want to confront the dealer with a written estimate from your garage stating that the repairs are not merely cosmetic, that the vehicle is dangerous and undrivable, and that the work is the minimum required to make it roadworthy and to pass the mandatory safety inspection. Include the price of a rental or courtesy car, mileage charges and taxes in your estimate. You can now go back to the dealer and present your case. Call first to make sure he will be there, and tell him a couple of problems have surfaced on which you would like his opinion.

Do not drive the car again in its present condition. Although the dealer is responsible for selling you an unfit vehicle, if you continue to use it and are stopped by the police, or have an accident, you may be held responsible for the consequences. If the dealer wishes to confirm the condition for himself, then he can visit the garage, pay to have it towed to his lot, or drive it back himself.

Before you confront the dealer, decide whether you want to keep the car and have it repaired at his expense, or whether you want a full refund. You might want to present him with the two alternatives and agree to accept the one he chooses, which will indicate some flexibility on your part, and may result in less hostility.

The dealer will undoubtedly produce his copy of the receipt and will insist that the disclaimer absolves him of any responsibility for what may be wrong with the car. You will have to convince him that you took him at his word when he told you the car was in good condition, and that since he has been proved wrong, you have been misled, unintentionally or not. Besides which, you have been sold goods that are not suitable for their intended purpose, and the "as is" disclaimer with no legal interpretation is not sufficient to justify such a transaction. You do not know how familiar the dealer is with his true legal position, but you can be sure that if he has been in business for some time, he knows from experience what he can get away with. You will have to make it clear that he has to choose one of the options you have given him, and that you are not prepared to compromise. Emphasize that you cannot drive the car because it is too dangerous for use on the public highway, and that he should go to the garage and see for himself. Offer to get a second opinion, if he doubts the validity of your estimate.

If all attempts to convince him that he has to meet your demands are met with absolute denial of responsibility, then you must tell him that you are not prepared to accept his protests, and that you will be informing him in writing immediately of the steps you are now obliged to take. You should then leave the dealership, decide which option is most acceptable to you, and write to the dealer with the details of what he must expect.

If you decide to return the car, you will be without transportation again, and will probably have to pay to have the vehicle towed back to the dealer. It may take some time to recover the $3,200, and meanwhile you may have to spend at least the same amount again for a replacement. Also, the $3,200 is over the limit for small claims, which means you will have to reduce your claim to the maximum permitted in your area or else file a claim through a higher court. The latter is not a barrier to legal arbitration, but the process is not as simple as small claims court, and you should check with the appropriate courts in your area for the procedure for filing a larger claim.

Although you will probably have to pay cash to the garage for the repairs, and it may be inconvenient to be out of pocket for a while, keeping the car is probably the better choice. You will not be without transportation since, while the repairs are being made, you will be using a rental car, and once the work is done, you will have the reliable vehicle you originally thought you were getting. You will save time searching for a replacement vehicle, and avoid the possibility of buying another "surprise." The amount you will be claiming is about $1,400.00 including the rental, and this amount will be within the limits of small claims court. The dealer will be aware that he might have had to pay for the car to be repaired anyway in order to make a sale, in which case he is more likely to refund your $1,400 than he might have been to refund the full purchase price had you decided to return the car. Besides which, he may still make a profit — you do not know how little he paid for the car when he acquired it.

Assuming that verbal negotiation has proved fruitless and you have decided to keep the car, you authorize the garage to go ahead with the repairs (since correspondence will likely take a few days and you will be charged for storage if you leave the car untouched pending the outcome of your dispute). You rent alternative transportation while the repairs are being done.

Now write to the dealer as follows:

---

23 Perrin Court
Long Acres
S3W 8T4

Shay Dee Auto Sales
911 Sump Avenue
Long Acres
S5Y 5W1

March 3, 1992

For the attention of Wat Arrek, Proprietor

Dear Mr. Arrek,

On February 29, 1992, I purchased from your establishment, in good faith, a 1985 Ratling Titanic, serial number VVBTH4U6534R367, for $3,200.00, which I paid in cash.

You specifically described the car on several occasions during our negotiations as being in good condition, trouble free, and in excellent shape. Having no reason to doubt your word, and relying on your expertise in such matters, I was convinced by your confidence and agreed to purchase the car. In order to ensure that the vehicle was legally roadworthy, I requested that you have the car inspected and certified.

You were reluctant to do this, and explained that I would have to pay extra for what I assumed should have been a routine procedure. However you assured me that the vehicle would pass inspection without any problems, and so I took your word and concluded our transaction accordingly.

I then drove the car to a licensed inspection station, The

Injerd Auto Garage Ltd., 12 Main Street, Long Acres, where the owner, Mr. Miles Perower, agreed to perform the required checks. Some hours later, Mr. Perower informed me that the car had failed the inspection for several reasons, and I was shocked to learn of the following serious problems:

- Badly rusted chassis, requiring extensive welding and new floor panels
- Two cut tires needing replacement
- A temporarily repaired muffler needing replacement
- Two ball joints on the front suspension worn out
- Both rear suspension springs broken.

The cost for repairing these defects in order to make the car legally safe is $1,280.00, plus $115.00 for a rental car for four days during the work, for a total of $1,395.00. Mr. Perower also advised that, because the vehicle is in such dangerous condition, I should not drive it until all these faults had been corrected.

On March 2, 1992, I presented you with these facts, and since you had sold me a vehicle that was totally unusable for the purpose for which it was intended, in contravention of consumer protection legislation, and that did not fit the description under which it was offered, I requested that the vehicle be repaired at your expense, or that the purchase price be refunded in full.

You refused on the grounds that the vehicle was bought "as is" and so you were not responsible for its condition once it left your premises. Despite your protest, I hold you entirely responsible for selling me a vehicle that failed to meet its advertised description and the legal safety requirements.

I have authorized The Injerd Auto Garage Ltd. to begin the necessary repairs at once, and I look to you for immediate settlement of their account, which totals $1,395.00. Kindly forward to my address your

remittance for this amount without delay. If you fail to
do so, further steps will be taken to ensure collection.

Yours sincerely,

Sue Togetrich

Encl.

c.c. Lisa Lorry, Minister of Transport
    Bill Zinflaytd, Minister of Consumer
      and Corporate Affairs
    Phil Estein, President, Automobile Dealers Association

As I have explained earlier in this chapter, you will have to do a little
homework to discover the organizations to whom copies of your letter
should be sent. If you are not sure which government department is most
likely to have greater influence over the dealer, send copies to them all! If
he doesn't respond, or offers a partial settlement that is unacceptable,
then you will have to send a final demand, with a photocopy of a completed summons, as described in a previous example and in chapter 10.
Write as follows:

---

23 Perrin Court
Long Acres
S3W 8T4

Shay Dee Auto Sales
911 Sump Avenue
Long Acres
S5Y 5W1

March 18, 1992

For the attention of Wat Arrek, Proprietor

Dear Mr. Arrek,

To date, I have received no response to my letter of
March 3, 1992, requiring you to pay for the essential

repairs to the dangerous and unroadworthy 1985 Ratling Titanic you sold me on February 29, 1992.

Repairs have now been completed to my satisfaction, and the car has passed the required safety inspection. Enclosed is the invoice for the necessary repairs, totaling $1,395.00, as per the estimate in my previous letter.

Please be aware that unless this amount is received by me in full by Thursday, April 2, 1992, a summons will be filed without further notice. For your information, I enclose a copy of the summons to be filed.

Perhaps I may expect to hear from you before April 2?

Yours sincerely,

Sue Togetrich

Encls.

c.c. Lisa Lorry, Minister of Transport
     Bill Zinflaytd, Minister of Consumer
       and Corporate Affairs
     Phil Estein, President, Automobile Dealers Association
     Luke Ouwte, President, Credit Bureau

Remember to add the credit bureau to your list of interested parties and send each party a copy of the letter only, not a copy of the summons.

The dealer should now clearly understand your determination to pursue your claim through all means at your disposal, and should be quite shaken by your quick action and tenacity. It is entirely possible that in his line of work, he is obliged to spend considerable time defending his reputation! The specter of a court appearance may unsettle him and you may receive an acceptable offer well before you have to file the claim. If further action is necessary, you should have all the evidence you need to prove your claim.

NEW CAR IS A LEMON

Most motorists spend their first few years on the road driving a variety of used cars purchased with funds diverted from student loans or with the leftovers of what their first employers amusingly describe as a salary! Ancient and weary cars exhaust their impoverished owners with their quirks and their unfailing tendency to expire whenever overstretched budgets can least accommodate any more endurance tests. What great joy, then, when after years of hard work and a successful campaign to deceive your bank, you arrange the financing of your first brand-new car, and banish the dark memories of constant breakdowns to the dim pages of never-to-be-repeated history.

Unfortunately, new cars can be as much trouble as used ones, especially mass-produced vehicles at the lower end of the price range. Manufacturers, in order to increase profits and stay competitive, pare the quality of the components down to the absolute minimum specification required to do a particular job and to last only for the duration of the warranty. If the engineers and accountants have combined their talents on a particular model, there are sure to be shortcomings in quality. These faults will inevitably appear and should be covered by the manufacturer's warranties.

The dealership and the manufacturer are entirely responsible for any defects that occur through no fault of your own. Should your new car display unwanted quirks, you must make your displeasure very clear. Any inconvenience or expenses you suffer as a result of these shortcomings should be kept to an absolute minimum. Conversely, any inconvenience or expenses to the dealer and manufacturer should be maximized! This will increase their motivation to turn you into a satisfied customer as soon as possible.

Don't let dealers and manufacturers dictate their terms to you. If you purchase a vehicle with a guarantee of three years and a life expectancy of ten years, then you have every right to expect it to perform accordingly. You likely purchased the car on the basis of advertisements claiming that it is the finest, fastest, best-looking, and most dependable vehicle the world has been privileged to glimpse. The car must live up to its description, or its perpetrators will have to suffer the consequences.

So make sure you receive full compensation each and every time you return your car to the dealership, and any warranty applicable to the part repaired or replaced must be renewed when the repair is completed. Note all items that need repairing and replacing, and as soon as they have been fixed, write to the maker and the dealer stating that you are registering a fresh warranty on the replacement parts, equal in years and/or distance to the one covering the original parts.

For example, say your engine fails. Then you would write to both the manufacturer and the dealer, as follows:

32 Chalk Road
Redemption
T4T 4F3

Doume & Gloume Auto Sales Ltd. & Armageddon Motors Ltd.
10 Cruquide Ave.   Great Bolzup
Redemption   Motoun
T2Y 9P1   M4R 7S6

February 21, 1992

For the attention of   &   For the attention of
Austin Tashous, President   Gerry Attrick, President

Dear Sirs,

On February 20, 1992, the engine of my 1992
Armageddon Perrish 4000 GT was replaced under
warranty at Dume & Gloume Auto Sales Ltd., after only
one month of normal use.

Since the car was covered with a warranty of three
years from new, the same conditions of warranty must
apply to all parts repaired or replaced during that period.

Kindly therefore ensure that your records of my vehicle
state that the new engine described above is guaranteed
for a full thirty-six months from the date of installation.
The vehicle serial number is 34684533AS8784FG12.

Yours sincerely,

Rick Shaw

What you are doing is pointing out to both parties that you are aware of their collective responsibility for your car, and that you will make a claim if necessary. If the new engine fails, and the maker and dealer "cannot find" their copies of your letter, your file copy and garage receipts establish a new warranty and prove you are entitled to further replacements, if needed. Send a similar letter for all repairs

If you are experiencing or anticipating numerous problems, compose a standard letter leaving the relevant details blank, make as many photocopies as you think you might need, and fill in the appropriate details as necessary. This way you will not be discouraged by the tedious correspondence necessary to make your point, and your service records at the dealer and manufacturer will soon swell to an impressive and very annoying magnitude!

Apart from making yourself a time-consuming, and therefore expensive, nuisance to the people responsible for the performance of your car, your unwelcome tenacity might ultimately have a further benefit. If you are unlucky enough to have bought a lemon — a vehicle with endless problems — you may be obliged to get the dealer to take it back and refund your money, a path he would not readily select. Since you have already proved to be his most frequent and least profitable customer, you might find him keen to listen to your proposals, if you promise never to come back again. Ever!

In addition, unless the repair can be fixed on the spot and quickly, you are entitled to alternative transportation. If the dealer does not have a courtesy car or is not willing to provide one, then you must rent one and invoice the dealership. In fact, you can give the dealer several options if taking your car in to the dealership disrupts your working day. He can arrange to have your car picked up and have a courtesy car left for you, or you will rent one yourself. He can stay open until you are able to deliver the car after work, or you will deliver it during your working day, and invoice him for the inconvenience and loss of income in addition to any rental expenses. After a few demonstrations of your technique, you will find him very keen indeed to make sure your car runs as smoothly as possible.

Don't allow the dealer to sway you with smooth assurances that the warranty doesn't cover rental cars, customer inconvenience and expenses, labor charges, or whatever else. If a part under warranty expires, its replacement must be covered, including labor. Had the part been adequately manufactured and installed in the first place, as should be expected in a new car, you would be happily driving the car instead of spending your valuable time in a repair shop.

Don't feel sorry for the salesman because he was so kind and helpful when you bought the car. All salesmen are kind and helpful — that is how they are able to sell things! Everyone leaves car showrooms wondering whether to invite the salesman over for dinner to celebrate their new friendship, while, back in his office, the salesman is gleefully patting himself on the back for having converted another hesitant and trusting customer into a commission!

And don't feel guilty because it's not the dealer's fault if the manufacturer sends him an occasional dud. No one forced him to be a dealer for that particular manufacturer. He is an expert on the makes he sells, and knows exactly how good or bad they are; he earns a great deal of money on every new vehicle he sells; and he, in turn, will be claiming his losses for repairs back from the makers. And he will be keeping his mechanics gainfully employed!

Let's say that, while driving along to work one fine day, your GT 4000 backfires, gives a shudder, and dies on the road. You call the dealer, but there is no reply. So you leave a conspicuous note on the dashboard explaining that the car has broken down and is awaiting a tow, leave a spare key in the glove compartment, make sure the car is fully locked, and take the most convenient method of transportation to work. If you take a taxi, don't forget to get a receipt from the driver.

When you arrive at work, you call the dealer again, and after explaining the events of the morning and where the car is, you ask him whether he will pick it up, or whether he would prefer you to make the arrangements and invoice him later. He tells you that he cannot provide a courtesy car unless he is given adequate notice, and that all his cars are in use. You repeat that you need a replacement car immediately, that you will rent one yourself, and present him with the bill as soon as your own car is satisfactorily repaired and returned. Remember to speak to the person with the highest authority — the president will do fine.

Having made your course of action perfectly clear, you then rent your replacement, and continue to use it until the dealer tells you that your own car is ready. It is up to the dealer to let you know when it is ready, but the longer it takes the dealer to repair your car, the greater will be his expense for a rental replacement. In this case your car is ready three days later. Over the phone, you ask what repairs were made so that you can fill out one of your extended warranty forms, which you will take with you when you go to collect the car. You should also prepare an invoice, including all reasonable expenses, that should look like this:

Rick Shaw
32 Chalk Road
Redemption
T4T 4F3

Dume & Gloume Auto Sales Ltd.
10 Cruquide Ave
Redemption
T2Y 9P1

February 28, 1992

For the attention of Austin Tashous, President

INVOICE

Re: Armageddon Perrish 4000 GT Serial number 56467876BW5634DQ78, purchased new on January 15, 1992.

For expenses incurred as a result of deprivation of
use of the above vehicle from 8:12 a.m. on February
25, 1992, to 7:00 p.m. on February 28, 1992, as
a result of premature failure and subsequent
replacement and repair of electrical wiring to
distributor. Repaired under 36-month warranty:
new 36-month warranty on repaired parts to
commence from date of job completion, per
enclosed registration statement dated February 28,
1992.

Taxi from breakdown site February 25, to workplace	$ 8.27
Loss of wages February 25, ¾ hour @ $28.50 per hour	21.37
Rental car from February 25 to February 28 (copy invoice enclosed)	125.87
Total this invoice	$155.51

Terms: Net monthly. Overdue accounts attract interest at
1.5% per month.

When you meet Mr. Tashous, or a colleague with the authority to make decisions, point out firmly and calmly that since the warranty covers the cost of replacing any faulty parts, it must also cover all damages resulting from the defect. Be clear that you are not going to back away from or reduce your claim, and ask him to authorize the payment. If he does not immediately reach for the Dume & Gloume checkbook, inform him that you will be including the unpaid invoice, together with a covering letter detailing your continuing disappointment in their products and service, to Armageddon Motors with the copy of the new warranty.

The next step is a letter to the president of Armageddon Motors, as follows:

32 Chalk Road
Redemption
T4T 4F3

Armageddon Motors Ltd.
Great Bolzup
Motoun
M4R 7S6

February 29, 1992

For the attention of Gerry Attrick, President

Dear Mr. Attrick,

I was so impressed by your many lavish and persuasive
television and newspaper advertisements highlighting the
performance and innumerable virtues of the Armageddon
Perrish 4000 GT, I was convinced that this must be the
car to fulfill all my needs, and on January 15, 1992, I
purchased a brand-new model from your authorized
dealer, Dume & Gloume Auto Sales Ltd., in my hometown
of Redemption.

The full purchase price of the car was $23,673.34,
and for this not inconsiderable sum, I confidently
anticipated that I might have several years of
comprehensively warrantied, trouble-free motoring,
as strongly emphasized in your advertising and
confirmed in glowing terms by your representatives
at Dume & Gloume Auto Sales. As a fellow
businessman, I know you will appreciate my extreme
disappointment and annoyance when my Perrish broke
down at an extremely inconvenient moment in my
working week, after less than two months. This is
hardly a glowing testimony to the accuracy of your
advertising.

The necessary repairs have now been completed, and
in view of this alarming example of premature
mechanical fragility, I would be very keen indeed to

receive your considered estimate of how often I am likely to experience further lamentable demonstrations of such unreliability. I would also appreciate your immediate settlement of the enclosed invoice for $155.51, covering my losses resulting from the breakdown.

Since the enclosed warranty covers all faults that arise as a consequence of faulty or defective parts or workmanship, it must, therefore, also include losses as a result of such failures incurred by the owner of the warranty. Messrs. Dume & Gloume have failed to grasp this important point, and I would be most grateful for your speedy remittance. I also enclose for your service records an updated statement of warranty, claiming a new 36-month guarantee on the replacement parts and labor.

I look forward to your early reply, and settlement of my invoice.

Yours sincerely,

Rick Shaw

Encls.

c.c. Austin Tashous, President, Dume & Gloume Auto
     Sales Ltd.

You send a copy to Mr. Tashous in the hope that he may be frightened into sending you a check and his abject apology at once. Furthermore it is good manners to keep him informed of your persistence and your lack of tolerance for shoddy treatment.

A reply may not be immediate, for there will undoubtedly be some discussion between the manufacturer and dealer before a decision can be arrived at, and acted upon.

If you have not received any response in say, ten days, a gentle reminder to the chairman should keep the ball rolling, and will keep you from getting too bored! Something along these lines should suffice:

32 Chalk Road
Redemption
T4T 4F3

Armageddon Motors Ltd.
Great Bolzup
Motoun
M4R 7S6

March 9, 1992

For the attention of Cy Lynderhead, Chairman

Dear Mr. Lynderhead,

On February 28, I was obliged to write to your president,
Gerry Attrick, concerning the appalling reliability of my
new automobile manufactured by your company, and the
consequent distress and financial loss I have suffered
through this experience.

Thus far, Mr. Attrick has not seen fit to address my
concerns, and I would be obliged if you could ensure that
either he or his successor takes immediate steps to settle
this outstanding matter. Please let me know by return
post that you have personally taken charge of this
unfortunate incident, and that it will be resolved to my
satisfaction without delay.

Thank you in anticipation.

Yours sincerely,

Rick Shaw

Note that you have deliberately given as few details of your complaint as
possible. This means that Mr. Lynderhead will have to interrupt his busy
schedule to get a copy of your letter from his president in order to understand the nature of the problem. The president should then be quite keen to
settle with you, and a quick response can be anticipated.

You will also have noted that a copy of this letter was not sent to the dealer. You don't want the dealer to know that your letter to the president went unanswered. In the remote possibility that your latest letter goes unanswered, too, then a final letter will be sent to the presidents of both the dealership and the manufacturer as follows:

---

32 Chalk Road
Redemption
T4T 4F3

Dume & Gloume Auto Sales Ltd. & Armageddon Motors Ltd.
10 Cruquide Avenue   Great Bolzup
Redemption   Motoun
T2Y 9P1   M4R 7S6

March 18, 1992

For the attention of   &   For the attention of
Austin Tashous, President   Gerry Attrick, President

Dear Sirs,

To date, my invoice of February 28, 1992, for $155.51, remains unpaid.

Your failure to accept responsibility for losses arising from the sale of faulty and unreliable goods is both deplorable and unacceptable, and will not be tolerated.

Unless full settlement is received by Monday, April 13, 1992, a summons will be filed citing both Dume & Gloume Auto Sales Ltd. and Armageddon Motors Ltd. without further notice.

Kindly govern yourselves accordingly.

Yours sincerely,

Rick Shaw

This should finally sway them, since a court appearance will be time consuming for both defendants, and the potential bad publicity most undesirable. If filing the claim becomes necessary, details of the appropriate procedure is covered in chapter 10.

If, as is most likely, your invoice is paid with little protest by either the maker or the dealer, or the amount is paid into court, or the court rules against the defendants, you will have established a precedent, which can be cited to expedite any further claims should your car continue to perform unreliably. Payment is interpreted as an admission of liability, and all subsequent claims will be subject to the same conditions, which will provide you with considerable leverage with both the manufacturer and the dealership.

If your car is repeatedly unreliable, you might consider demanding a complete refund of the purchase price. If such drastic action becomes necessary, having written evidence for all repairs, sending new warranty statements, and collecting compensation for incurred financial losses will be to your advantage. The dealer may be quite amenable to negotiating a reimbursement if he weighs it against the continuing expense and inconvenience of dealing with you. He already knows that your demands cannot be treated lightly.

If you do decide that enough is enough, that you are fed up watching your vehicle heading off into the sunset attached to the business end of a towtruck, then you must collect all your evidence, and arrange to meet Mr. Tashous. By now you should know him quite well, so a verbal discussion is quite in order and, if conducted civilly, will not prejudice any further written exchange that may be required. Arrange all your invoices and expenses in chronological order, and then list them on a separate sheet of paper, totaling the various inconveniences under appropriate subheadings, including the approximate cost of each repair had it not been completed under warranty. This will emphasize the amount of money that Dume & Gloume or the manufacturer is losing by keeping the vehicle on the road.

Make the list look comprehensive and professional — it may need to be used in court.

Record of repairs to Armageddon Perrish 4000 GT, Serial Number 56467876BW5634DQ78, purchased new on January 15, 1992, from Dume & Gloume Auto Sales Ltd. by Rick Shaw.

July 31, 1992

Date & Repair	Cost of Repairs	Expenses Paid to Owner
February 28, 1992 New BotchAmp electronic management system, and distributor wiring	$ 973.00	$155.51
April 14, 1992 New transmission	1,536.00	203.65
May 4, 1992 New power steering	1,134.00	101.54
etc.		
7 breakdowns/repairs	$6,342.00	$873.89
Total cost	$7,215.89	

Present the list and suggest that the theoretical costs of running the car so far amount to $13,321.64 annually. Emphasize that at that rate, in two years the amount spent will have exceeded the original purchase price by $2,969.94! Furthermore, since each time a repair or replacement has been executed you have registered a fresh warranty for a further 36 months, the potential expenses are likely to continue for a very long time indeed. Point out that you intend to keep the vehicle for at least eight years.

Mention that you sympathize with Mr. Tashous's position, of course, and confirm that you appreciate the cooperation and service he has provided over the months, but despite the friendship that has built up through your frequent visits to his establishment, you must insist that you be relieved of the burden of owning the recalcitrant vehicle. As a demonstration of your unflagging devotion to fair-mindedness and flexibility, offer him a choice of how to refund your money. Your preference would be for the dealership to give you a complete refund of the purchase price. Or, if this is not convenient, you will sell the car yourself, and look to the dealer for the difference between the original price paid and the amount realized from the secondhand sale, plus any additional expenses incurred for advertising the car.

Of course, it is only fair to mention that, should you have to sell the car yourself, as an honest and considerate person, you will be under a moral and legal obligation to accurately describe to potential buyers the problems you have experienced during your ownership.

You should find the dealer most cooperative, but he will probably not want to seem too eager to capitulate. You may need to let him think it over for a day or two. He will by then have weighed the situation carefully, and have consulted with the manufacturer. Should he not be persuaded by your argument, then you will have to confirm your intentions in a letter to both the dealer and the manufacturer as follows:

---

32 Chalk Road
Redemption
T4T 4F3

Dume & Gloume Auto Sales Ltd.	&	Armageddon Motors Ltd.
10 Cruquide Avenue		Great Bolzup
Redemption		Motoun
T2Y 9P1		M4R 7S6

August 4, 1992

For the attention of	&	For the attention of
Austin Tashous, President		Gerry Attrick, President

Dear Sirs,

Further to my conversation with Mr. Austin Tashous on Friday, July 31, 1992 concerning the continuing lack of reliability of my Armageddon Perrish 4000 GT, serial number 56467876BW5634DQ78, purchased January 15, 1992, from Dume & Gloume Auto Sales Ltd., I confirm herewith that I am no longer prepared to endure the unacceptable burden of ownership of this vehicle.

Enclosed is a list of the faults that have plagued the car from the time of purchase to the present date, which is excessive for any form of transportation, let alone a car that was purchased brand-new.

Should the unreliability continue at its present rate, the cost of repairs and resulting expenses will amount to $13,321.64 per annum. Since I normally keep a car for about eight years, and since I am registering a new 36-month warranty after every breakdown, you may expect to lose the sum of $106,573.12 during the lifetime of the vehicle. Furthermore, my daughter will be using the car to drive to her new job, which is some distance out of town, and I am not prepared to risk her safety should the car break down at night or far from assistance. Any additional expenses incurred through renting a replacement vehicle and repairs by a local garage, if required, would considerably increase the estimates described above.

Kindly confirm, therefore, that you will make the necessary arrangements to cancel my purchase contract, take back the car, and refund in full the purchase price of $23,673.34 without delay.

In the event you are not prepared to comply with my claim, please be advised that I will have no alternative but to sell the vehicle myself and look to you for the difference between the amount realized and the original purchase price. My legal and moral obligation to disclose the number and frequency of repairs experienced to date to any prospective purchaser will no doubt adversely influence the price the car might sell for, which will be reflected in the balance I shall be seeking in compensation.

I look forward to your immediate proposals.

Yours sincerely,

Rick Shaw

Encl.

If the car was purchased on credit, it may not be practicable to sell privately and claim the balance. If this is the case, delete the paragraph "In the event . . . seeking in compensation."

If neither of your proposals is accepted, you will have to decide which option is most convenient and give the manufacturer and dealer final notice of your intention. If you need to seek legal redress through the courts, the amount claimed will exceed the small claims limit whichever option you select, and you will need to seek legal advice. Incidentally, if you are still making monthly payments on the car, don't be tempted to stop the payments — apart from the risk of repossession, your wanting to return the car could be interpreted as your inability to make payments. Also, you should not return the car until the matter is resolved, so that you still have the "evidence," should it be required for any reason, and you still have transportation.

If you have decided to return the car rather than sell it, write a final letter as follows:

---

32 Chalk Road
Redemption
T4T 4F3

Dume & Gloume Auto Sales Ltd.   &   Armageddon Motors Ltd.
10 Cruquide Avenue   Great Bolzup
Redemption   Motoun
T2Y 9P1   M4R 7S6

August 13, 1992

For the attention of   &   For the attention of
Austin Tashous, President   Gerry Attrick, President

Dear Sirs,

Further to my letter dated August 4, 1992, in which I gave notice that my 1992 Armageddon Perrish 4000 GT was so appallingly unreliable that I had no option but to return it for complete reimbursement of the purchase price of $23,673.34.

I am disappointed to learn that you are not prepared to take back the car and refund my money. I therefore must inform you that in order to satisfy my claim, a summons for the full amount plus costs will be filed without further notice, unless full settlement is received by Monday, September 7, 1992.

I am sure you are aware that the publicity generated by this action could affect future sales. I trust you share my interest in ensuring that any such publicity does not become necessary, and look forward to your taking appropriate preventive measures before the above date.

I shall maintain possession of the vehicle in question, pending the decision of the court.

Yours sincerely,

Rick Shaw

c.c. Cy Lynderhead, Chairman, Armageddon Motors Ltd.

Sending a copy to the chairman will ensure that all parties are aware of what is about to be initiated and have the opportunity to preempt your action.

It is possible that you will not be offered a full refund since you have had use of the car for some months. You should be flexible if you think it will expedite a speedy settlement. But be firm, and insist on a figure close to the full amount. If you are not offered a satisfactory settlement, then the summons will have to be filed (See chapter 10).

Or you might want to delay court action for a while longer in the hope that a few more expensive repairs will convince the dealer that he should take the car back. If you choose this route, and subsequently have to file the summons, you are not obliged to inform the dealer again of your intentions since you already stated that you will act without further notice.

4

Till Death Do Us Part: Insurance Woes

Insurance is a reluctant necessity, and even if you are fortunate enough to live from cradle to grave without making a claim, the premiums are gone forever!

UNJUSTIFIED RATE INCREASE

Insurance renewal time is rarely an occasion for hilarity and spontaneous celebration: premiums increase with monotonous regularity, usually with no explanation or justification. If you have an excellent claim record, which logic would dictate should result in a *reduction* in premiums, this can be very irritating. Unfortunately, your unblemished record generally fails to impress those responsible for deciding how much you can afford to pay! A slight increase over the rate of inflation can be justified, and sometimes even a large increase; you might, for instance, own a rare car that has increased sharply in value over the past year. On the other hand, if your premium is substantially higher for no apparent reason, you should seek a reduction.

Insurers and brokers make it their business to know the value of the goods they insure: you should make it yours, too. A diligent insurer will be aware of any factors that could affect your premiums: a sharp increase in burglaries in your neighborhood or a new railway line that could pose a potential hazard. An increase in property value, due to high demand, however, should not affect premiums since the cost of repairs does not change even if the land value does rise. New risks do justify a higher rate, but you should ensure that any increase is applied only to that portion of the policy to which it is applicable. For instance, a fifteen percent increase in break-ins in your town over the last year should mean that only the theft portion of your home insurance should be increased fifteen percent.

Most insurance must be purchased through independent brokers, and renewal notices from your broker are usually accompanied by a letter stating that the new premiums were compared with those offered by alternative companies and were found to be competitive. This may be true, but you are hardly in a position to judge. It is unlikely that a broker would have the time to compare premiums every time a policy is due for renewal. Therefore you should compare your rates with at least one other broker or insurance company each year. Your savings may be substantial.

Let us assume that you live in a modest apartment building in a thriving and industrious city, and that you regularly insure the contents of your apartment, which includes such items as a television and VCR, a microwave oven, and some jewelry bequeathed by a departed aunt. You have been insured by the same company for seven years, through a local broker, and have never made a claim of any kind. Last year the premium was assessed at $211.67, and the year before it was $192.84. The increase was certainly in excess of inflation, but still reasonable.

This year, the renewal notice arrives ten weeks before the due date so that the insurance company can have your money in its possession for as long as possible. (And it works! Most customers pay quickly "just to be on the safe side.") The premium is $253.78, or up more than twenty percent over last year, with no explanation whatsoever from the broker or the principal. You are surprised since you have not made a claim or altered the terms of coverage in any way. So what should you do?

Initially, a call to the broker will do no harm and might well result in an immediate, satisfactory explanation. However, in this case your agent tries to placate you with bland and imprecise reasons for the high premium, which include an increased number of claims, the high cost of replacing stolen or damaged goods, the escalation of crime in inner cities, and so forth. Naturally, you are not impressed since the broker is unable to furnish any viable statistics that might give the increase some credibility. The agent assures you that the premium is still competitive and that rates have gone up throughout the insurance industry for the reasons just offered.

This explanation is unsatisfactory and clearly demonstrates which client is more important to the agent: the insurance company. Having learned little from the broker, you should now confront the insurers directly. But before doing so, give the broker the benefit of the doubt, and call two other agencies for quotes, just in case all insurance companies have indeed put up their rates.

A few telephone calls later, you have quotes for identical insurance that range from $182.75 to $215.00. At this stage, you could switch your business to a new company, but you might want to stay with your present insurers because they are particularly reputable when it comes to settling claims. Better the devil you know . . .

The renewal date is still several weeks ahead, so you have plenty of time to decide. Meanwhile you could discover that your present company had made a "mistake," if pressed with sufficient conviction! However, it is vital to handle the dispute in a businesslike manner, and to maintain existing insurance or commence consecutive new insurance. Insurers cannot be relied upon to continue extended coverage while money is owed on unpaid premiums, even while a difference of opinion is under negotiation. And the insurer, who is always firmly on top of matters, could notify you that your policy has been canceled.

In this case, armed with the knowledge that lower rates are readily available elsewhere, it is time to convey your reluctance to pay more than necessary to your insurer as follows:

911 Steel Avenue
Apartment 403
Mediocher City
A5X 2A9

Graspp Fearcely Insurance Inc.
Babel Towers
Gratinkum
R4U LOT

October 4, 1991

For the attention of Robin Pillidge, President

Dear Mr. Pillidge,

I have been privileged to enjoy insurance coverage (Policy #GFI 3478623/6478) provided by your company for seven years, and purchased through your agents, Messrs. Harp, Gripe, & Mone Insurance Brokers Inc., of 43 Titannic Street, Mediocher City. During this time, I have always experienced courteous and efficient service from both you and your agents, and have been pleased with the competitive rates offered.

I was therefore surprised and shocked to see that my new premium has been increased by twenty percent, to $253.78, with no explanation for this unexpectedly high amount.

My records will show that I have never made a claim of any kind, that my status has not altered since beginning coverage seven years ago, and that I have always paid due premiums on demand.

I called my representative at Harp, Gripe, & Mone, a Mr. Harry Hopelis, who offered various vague possibilities by way of an explanation, none of which appeared to carry much conviction. Mr. Hopelis assured me that the new premium was still competitive. In order to verify his statement, I checked with some of your competitors. All five quotations were considerably less than the new premium required by your organization, and in fact, two of the quotes were for less than last year's premium!

I can only assume, therefore, that an error has occurred in the assessment of my new premium, and I should be most grateful if you could look into this at once, and let me know the correct amount at your earliest convenience.

In view of our mutually compatible relationship over the past seven years, I am naturally anxious it should continue uninterrupted, and I feel sure you would not want my business to be given to any of the several competitors who are apparently keen to offer a more attractive proposition than your own good organization.

I look forward to receiving details of my revised premium soon, and thank you in anticipation.

Yours sincerely,

Joan Ovvark

c.c. Harp, Gripe, & Mone

A copy of the letter was sent to the brokers as a courtesy, and to indicate to them that their performance has scarcely created a favorable impression.

Note that, in order to avoid leading the insurer into what could be a protracted and complex analysis of crime statistics, inflation's effect on the cost of damage repairs and so forth, no request for the reasons for the increase has been made. This way you avoid having to dispute those parts of the explanation you disagree with. Instead, you are merely pointing out to the insurer that his rates are seriously out of line with the competition's and that if he wants to keep your patronage, he now has the opportunity to appease you by correcting an unfortunate miscalculation by one of his subordinates. If he does reduce the premium, then the exercise will have been successful with very little exertion from you.

On the other hand, the insurer may provide a logical explanation for the increase, and you will achieve little through further correspondence. Since better rates are available and since initiating a new policy is a fairly painless operation, you would then be well advised to take your business elsewhere.

However, a parting shot will do no harm, and just might result in a change of heart or change of policy, if I may be allowed an unintentional pun! A final letter, such as the one following, will inform the insurance company that its rates are responsible for losing your valuable custom. If enough clients voice their opinion, perhaps the company will take notice, which will at least benefit future customers.

---

911 Steel Avenue
Apartment 403
Mediocher City
A5X 2A9

Graspp Fearcely Insurance Inc.
Babel Towers
Gratinkum
R4U LOT

October 24, 1991

For the attention of Robin Pillidge, President

Dear Mr. Pillidge,

I have received your letter dated October 22, replying to my request for the premium on my insurance policy #GFI 3478623/6478 to be reduced to a realistic level.

I have read your reasons for justifying such an exorbitant increase, and I am unable to accept your explanation.

Kindly be aware, therefore, that as of the expiry date of my policy, December 31, 1991, I shall be insuring with one of your numerous competitors, who is still able to offer coverage at reasonable and competitive rates.

Yours sincerely,

Joan Ovvark

c.c. Harp, Gripe, & Mone

Realistically, this is probably the best that can be done. Whatever the outcome, you are in a position to obtain a lower insurance rate.

PROPERTY DAMAGE NOT COVERED

The most valuable item the majority of people will ever insure is their home. But a house can be a complex and demanding possession, and the owner will undoubtedly be liable for a plethora of problems and repairs.

Comprehensive insurance coverage is essential, and great care must be taken to ensure that your policy specifically covers the property for all the eventualities that might befall it — exclusions or vague definitions can be ruinously expensive. Read your policy carefully, and make a note of anything you don't understand. Insurance terminology is geared, accidentally or deliberately, to completely baffle the insured, and it is usually no challenge to find clauses that are vague, contradictory, or open to subjective interpretation.

Happily, in cases where policy holders have had to resort to the courts, judges have been inclined to side with the insured in disputes involving obscure terminology, ruling that the average householder cannot be expected to have the experience and education of both a lawyer and an insurance representative. Although this is reassuring, prevention is better than cure.

You should make a list of all the eventualities that need to be covered, and have your insurer or broker tailor a policy to your needs. Since even made-to-measure policies are likely to contain vague clauses, before signing or accepting the document, you might also request a covering letter that itemizes your requirements and confirms where each item is included in the policy if you are in any doubt.

As you make your list, walk around your house and grounds, noting all the accidents and incidents that might happen over a lifetime. Don't leave out anything, no matter how bizarre or unlikely. Use a fresh page for each of the seasons; every season has its potential hazards, and unless you specifically think yourself into the appropriate time of year, you may miss a necessary item. On a hot August day, for instance, you might forget that your roof could cave in during an unexpectedly heavy snowfall in the middle of a January night, or that your basement could be flooded during a spring thaw.

Imagine the reasons your insurer might cite for refusing to pay a claim. Suppose your letter carrier steps on a loose or rotten tread on your front steps and is injured: the insurer might claim that you were negligent in maintaining your property and deny any liability. But what if the step had rotted from underneath, where water had been trapped between the tread and the stringer, out of sight and quite unknown to you? Would this still be interpreted as improper maintenance? Or suppose the letter carrier was injured on your property by a brick falling from a chimney on the house next door. Your neighbors have no insurance, and dispute their liability because the carrier was not on their property. Would your coverage be sufficient to indemnify you?

Or perhaps you and your family decide to visit relatives in Australia, and in view of the distance and expense, opt to make a marathon of it and stay for three months. In order to defray your daunting expenses, you rent the house while you are absent to a neighbor's relatives who happen to be on an extended visit to your town. If they accidentally flood the basement, causing considerable damage, will the insurers reject your claim because your coverage is for a private residence and not a rental property?

The possibility of any accident or loss, no matter how unlikely, should not be overlooked. Like any other business, an insurance company operates to make a profit, and even the most reputable organization may refuse to honor a claim if in its opinion the policy holder was negligent, or the coverage is insufficient to accommodate a particular loss.

Check with friends and colleagues who have similar insurance needs to yours; learn from their experiences. Have they encountered settlement problems? This information will guide you in deciding which insurance company best meets your particular requirements. Personal recommendations are worth far more than glib promises of life everlasting from the insurers' friendly, caring representative looming reassuringly into your living room from a television screen!

If you have the misfortune of having to make a claim, remember to perform all the duties that are generally prescribed in the policy, or accompanying instructions. Admit nothing, apologize to no one, say or do nothing that could be interpreted as an admission of liability. Call the appropriate emergency services, if required, and while waiting for their arrival, do whatever you can to prevent further damage to life or property, providing your own safety is not put at unnecessary risk, e.g., turn off the water supply in the case of a flood.

You should obtain the names and addresses of any witnesses, and make notes and drawings, or take photographs of any evidence you feel is necessary to substantiate your claim. This may be particularly useful if the damage or loss has to be repaired before the adjusters can arrive to verify a claim. A broken pane in a patio door used by small children, for instance, would obviously have to be repaired at once, in order to prevent even more serious loss through injury. The repairmen could also be contacted by the insurers if necessary.

If you have valuable possessions, such as antiques, paintings, or jewelry, make sure they are identified to the insurers, and that you have a record of any serial numbers or other characteristics, or photographs, which could confirm their loss, and possible recovery if stolen.

Inform the insurers or broker of any loss as soon as possible, even if it is a weekend — many insurers have an emergency number. Keep the number where all members of the family will have ready access to it. When you call to register a claim, note the date and time, and the name of the person to whom you speak. Ask the representative for specific instructions on what to do next, i.e., you may be required to call your agent during office hours or to confirm in writing, and so on. Make sure you carry out instructions to the letter.

When the adjuster arrives, you will probably have to fill out a claim form, which is usually a simple task. But if you feel you need to add further information in the form of drawings, photographs, or notes, by all means do so. If the claim is straightforward and the loss is adequately covered, settlement should be reached within a few days.

On the other hand, how should you proceed if your insurers reject a claim on the grounds that the loss is not covered under the terms of your policy?

Let's assume that you live in a modest two-story house. At the end of a long day, you like to rest your weary bones on a water bed, which you purchased new two years ago. You have obeyed its care and maintenance instructions scrupulously from the day of acquisition, and as a consequence, this wonderful invention has performed reliably.

However, you arrive home one evening to find pandemonium. Your previously unimpeachable water bed has become spontaneously and terminally incontinent; its aquatic stuffing has traveled across the bedroom floor, and has found its way to the living room below, accompanied by large chunks of plaster. Despite the frantic efforts of your spouse and two children to stem the flow of water and clean up the mess, the damage is still considerable — carpets, ceiling, walls, furniture, television, VCR — all have absorbed a generous amount of the water bed's lifeblood.

Once you have stopped the leak and completed the emergency mop-up operation to prevent any further damage, you call the insurance broker to tell him the good news. He offers his sympathy and promises that an adjuster will call you at your office the next morning. Having done your duty, you then drain the rest of the water from the offending bed, resurrect the original *vin ordinaire* mattress for the night, and take the family out to dinner in compensation for the unexpected adventure.

Next day, the adjuster calls your office to make an appointment to assess the damage, and appears at your home that evening as promised. You present your list of the structural, cosmetic, and contents damage, and she in turn gives you a statement of claim to complete for the insurers. After a tour of the damaged site, a few more questions, the adjuster tells you she will make a report to the insurance company, and leaves with the filled-out claim form.

Two days later, you receive a call from your broker. He says he has been instructed to ask whether you informed the insurers that you had installed a water bed, as there is no record of it in their copy of the policy. You are of course stunned to hear such a question, and reply that as far as you are aware, you were under no obligation to notify them of such a purchase, and assumed that such a commonplace item would not require any additional insurance. The broker says he will get back to you, and you hurry home to examine your policy.

After studying the fine print for some time, you verify that the building and contents are definitely covered against water damage, whether from internal or external causes. There is no specific clause that covers damage from a water bed; indeed there is no mention of water beds anywhere in the policy nor in any of the various renewal notices and other correspondence from the insurers over the years.

Two days later, a letter arrives from the insurance company explaining that water beds are considered an additional risk, over and above normal beds, that the company requires written notification of any such furniture, and that the relevant premium will be adjusted upwards accordingly. Furthermore, since the item causing the loss was not covered, the insurer is unable to assume responsibility and settle the claim.

Dumbstruck, you call the broker to seek his opinion, and he sadly confirms that some insurers do indeed require additional premiums for water beds. He informs you that in his opinion all you can do is pay for the damage yourself and make sure that in future your insurance covers water beds.

You now have three options: you can pursue the insurance company, the manufacturer of the water bed, or both. Your case against the insurers is fairly good, since their policy does not specifically exclude water beds. Your policy definitely covers water damage, which is what you have suffered. If insurers are wary of water beds, and require additional coverage, they, as the experts, should convey that information to their clients in writing or through a specific clause in the policy. Should the insurance company refuse to settle, then the bed manufacturer should at least refund the price of the bed or provide you with a replacement (see the next chapter on tackling the retailers). Or you can initiate proceedings against both parties simultaneously. But since you cannot reasonably or legally expect to be paid by them both, you begin by pursuing the insurance company.

---

843 Fludd Street
Notarrid
W8T 0C4

Knott Ourfawlt Insurance Ltd.
Parsimoneous Building
Welheeld
F3S 0W3

October 19, 1991

For the attention of Des Picabell, President

Dear Mr. Picabell,

I hold several insurance policies, all issued by your good offices through Messrs. Braak, Swerv, Skidde, & Impakt Insurance Brokers Ltd., and which include Policy #5545/HL1289 covering my house and its contents.

On October 10, 1991, my property sustained water damage through leakage from a water bed in the master bedroom. My family and I were able to stop the leak and mop up as best we could, but the damage was still sufficient to necessitate a claim under the terms of the policy mentioned above. I informed my broker that same evening, and the loss was confirmed the next day by your adjuster.

I have now received a letter from your offices stating that you decline to settle my claim on the grounds that my coverage does not specify water bed indemnity. The policy in question has been in effect for more than fifteen years. It was purchased because it was the most comprehensive coverage offered by your organization, and because I was under the impression that you are insurers of the highest repute — an image that is consistently emphasized in your advertising.

I have examined my policy and it is abundantly clear in section A, part 3, that the property and contents are covered against all types of water damage, from both external and internal sources. There is no mention of any item or event, let alone specific mention of water beds, that is excluded from this coverage. Therefore, by your own definition, which is quite unambiguous, I am clearly covered for the loss for which I am seeking due settlement.

I appreciate that mistakes can occur, even in a business of your long standing and reputation, and I am sure I can rely on you to resolve this matter quickly. I am advised that in circumstances of this nature, the opinion of Mr. Yasser Nosur, at the Federal Insurance Bureau, can be most helpful. If you wish me to refer the matter to him, I would be happy to comply with your instructions.

I look forward to your immediate reply.

Yours sincerely,

Kal Amity

c.c. Braak, Swerv, Skidde, & Impakt Insurance Brokers Ltd.

You have refrained from accusing the insurers of skulduggery and have merely suggested that an error must have occurred, which gives them the opportunity to save face. The gentle sting in the tail, mentioning the president of the Federal Insurance Bureau, shows that you have done your homework. You have not mentioned in the letter that Mr. Nosur is the president, since Mr. Picabell will know this, but he will, of course, be aware from the tone of your letter that you know it, too. In the unlikely event of further refusal to settle, then a firm response will be required, as follows:

843 Fludd Street
Notarrid
W8T 0C4

Knott Ourfawlt Insurance Ltd.
Parsimoneous Building
Welheeld
F3S 0W3

October 25, 1991

For the attention of Klauz Invallid, Chairman

Dear Mr. Invallid,

I am in receipt of a letter from your president, Mr. Des Picabell, dated October 23, 1991, confirming that your company is not prepared to settle my claim of October 10, 1991, in breach of contract clearly defined in my policy #5545/HL1289.

I trust that I can rely on your making the consequences of such ill-advised business ethics quite apparent to Mr. Picabell, by letting him know that unless I receive full settlement by Tuesday, November 5, 1991, a court summons will be filed without further notice.

Yours sincerely,

Kal Amity

c.c. Braak, Swerv, Skidde, & Impakt Insurance Brokers Ltd.
     Yasser Nosur, President, Federal Insurance Bureau

Send copies of your correspondence to the Insurance Bureau with a separate covering letter.

---

843 Fludd Street
Notarrid
W8T 0C4

Federal Insurance Bureau
Lymprist Building
Lastrizort Street
Capitol City
B2G 4K3

October 25, 1991

For the attention of Yasser Nosur, President

Dear Mr. Nosur,

As you will see from the enclosed correspondence, I am obliged to file a summons in order to obtain due and just settlement from a company that is presumably subject to regulations imposed and policed by the organization over which you preside.

Please let me know by return post that Knott Ourfawlt Insurance Ltd. will be subject to immediate and thorough inspection and audit by your office, with your findings made public in order that other innocent policy holders may be spared the injustice I am currently experiencing.

Yours sincerely,

Kal Amity

Encls.

c.c. Klauz Invallid, Chairman, and Des Picabell, President,
    Knott Ourfawlt Insurance Ltd.
    Braak, Swerv, Skidde, & Impakt Insurance Brokers Ltd.

You have carefully avoided asking the Insurance Bureau to intervene on your behalf. Instead, you have given the impression that you are quite capable of obtaining satisfaction through the courts, and that such action is almost routine and requires no special effort on your part. The copies will convey the same impression to the chairman and president, which will leave them in no doubt that you are determined to carry out your promised action, no matter what.

Copies of everything should be sent to your brokers, who may help persuade the insurers to capitulate; your broker may reconsider doing business with the insurers in the future, a fact that might tip the scale in your favor.

Few companies will not readily yield under this kind of pressure, and you should soon receive a check in full settlement. If not, file the summons, as described in Chapter 10.

FAULTY REPAIR BY INSURANCE COMPANY CONTRACTOR

Once an insurance claim is settled, arrangements must be made to repair or replace the property damaged, lost, or stolen. Inevitably, insurers prefer to appoint their own contractors in order to keep costs down, and they may be tempted to select contractors whose rates and workmanship are considerably below the industry norm. The shareholders of the insurance company may be happy, but for the claiming householder who experiences the workmanship demonstrated by such contractors, this could prove to be a character-building adventure. However, as in the case of car insurance, policy holders are entitled to obtain estimates for repairs from independent contractors of their own choosing and to insist on a check in settlement, which they can spend on the repairs or however they choose.

Repairs to a house can be complicated, and many homeowners are unwilling to risk appointing a contractor themselves. They may be afraid of the potential nightmare if all does not go according to plan or of calling contractors and subcontractors back to correct faulty work; they may lack the knowledge to check that a job is being done properly; or they may be unwilling to assume the responsibility for a job that could have been handled by the insurance company.

Obtaining your own contractors has its advantages: you can select a contractor who you know does good work; you have more control over materials; and you can use the cash settlement from the insurers at your discretion. In any case, it is good to obtain independent quotes in order to understand the costs and work involved in the repairs. You should obtain three quotes, which you should present to the insurer.

Let us assume, then, that your kitchen has been severely damaged by fire. Since rebuilding a kitchen is complex and requires a number of subcontractors, and since you urgently need your kitchen, you decide to leave the repairs entirely in the hands of the insurers. There will, of course, be forms to fill out; any form that you are required to sign should be read carefully to ensure that you are not depriving yourself of any rights.

You may also be required to complete a form that gives the insurers the right to decide whether the completed job is satisfactory. Unfortunately, most insurance documentation is completely standardized, and you will not be allowed to alter any of the clauses you disagree with. And until you do agree to all the conditions, the insurer will simply not process your claim. This puts you in an unenviable position; if you are in a hurry you may have no choice but to comply. However, compliance does not necessarily mean that you are waiving your rights completely, providing you take, and record, steps to give yourself some backup protection.

Suppose you are asked to sign a waiver that contains the clauses "The insured authorizes the Company to effect all necessary repairs entirely at their discretion" and "The Company's decision in assessing the satisfactory completion is final and binding." You should request that they be deleted or altered so that your opinion concerning the quality of the completed job is taken into account. Your request will be refused, but at least you will have a record of your objection. Record the place, date, time and the full name and title of the person to whom you make the request. If you have witnesses, so much the better.

You should ask the representative to clarify the meaning of these clauses. He will probably inform you that the clauses are just there to protect the company and that, of course, your opinion will be taken into account. Get him to contradict the meaning and intention of the clauses as comprehensively as possible and write down the terminology he uses. State clearly that you still wish the clauses to be deleted, but that since he refuses to do so, and you have no option, you will sign the authorization in light of his verbal assurances. Then sign the form, and check your notes to make sure you have recorded everything in the discussion.

Insurers do have a valid point in wanting to include clauses that give them as much authority as possible to oversee how their money is spent, and one should not automatically assume that they are out to shortchange their customers. These clauses seem to favor the insurers, but they are entitled to some contractual protection against unreasonable clients.

Once the work is started, it is up to you to police the operation and to notify the contractor (not his subcontractors or employees) of any problems.

You should inform the insurer, too — verbally at first, but if nothing is done to correct the disputed work, confirm it in writing.

Do your inspection after the workmen have gone at the end of the day. Don't assume that something is wrong because it doesn't look quite right, particularly when the roughing-in is being done. It is normal, for example, for tradesmen to make alarmingly large and irregular holes to accommodate various fixtures, holes that will later be covered by drywall or tiles. If you are not sure about something, get a second opinion.

In your case, the job has progressed reasonably well, and should be finished in a day or two. Today, the new cabinets are to be installed. At four-thirty in the afternoon, you receive a frantic call at your office from your spouse, who tells you that the cabinets are nothing like the ones they are replacing and that they appear not even to fit properly. Filled with apprehension, you head for home.

Sure enough, the cabinets are nothing like the originals: the hinges and handles are different; one section finishes six inches short of a wall it should butt against; and the upper set is not level but follows the ceiling line, which has sagged toward the center of the house over the years. To add insult to injury, the surfaces have been scratched by the installers.

Fortunately, the contractor is still there, and you quickly point out the deficiencies to him. He replies that these are the cabinets authorized by the insurers, that he has merely followed instructions, that the scratches are "hardly anything," and that the cabinets destroyed in the fire were probably much worse. As for the installation, the contractor claims the cabinets are close to level and that it is not unusual for installers to use the ceiling as a guide. He suggests you contact the insurance company.

The next morning, the insurance representative informs you that since the contractor will be finished that afternoon, he will be dropping by to make a final inspection of the work anyway. But when you arrive home, you discover that the cabinets are exactly as they were, although the work appears completed and all the contractors and equipment have gone.

A call to the insurance office reveals that the representative did call to make a final inspection, as promised, and that he thought the job, cabinets included, was perfectly adequate. You point out again, in detail, the reasons why you disagree, but he reaffirms that as far as his company is concerned, the claim has now been settled in full.

Further discussion is obviously not going to produce results, so a letter to the insurers must be dispatched without delay. Though your contract is with the insurers and not the contractor, you should keep him abreast of all that transpires between you and the insurers so that he cannot later claim he was unaware of any dispute. Your first letter should be as follows:

45 Perrel Avenue
Gullibal
D3G 6Q2

Pulla, Faastwun Insurance Inc.
Ethix-Notus Towers
Pirana
B3N 8M7

October 21, 1991

For the attention of Penny Wise, President

Dear Ms. Wise,

Claim # 75531/RT

Further to my telephone conversation this morning
with your Mr. Arie Gant, and his appointed contractor,
Mr. Ahmad Mann, of Cloke & Dagah Construction Ltd.,
I regret that the replacement cabinets in my kitchen
are entirely unsatisfactory, for the following
reasons:

- The surface material on the old cabinets was Arbor-
  ite; the replacement material is melamine.
- The new hinges are not fully adjustable, and do not
  permit sufficient movement to facilitate accurate
  door alignment.
- The new door handles are nothing like the original
  solid oak pulls.
- One upper section finishes six inches short of a
  wall — the original set fitted exactly.
- Neither upper set is level. They have been aligned to
  the ceiling, which has sagged over the years.
- The exposed surfaces are visibly scratched.

In view of the otherwise professional job executed
courteously and quickly by Mr. Mann and his crew, and
the prompt and considerate settlement processed by Mr.

Gant, I can only assume that perhaps the supplier of the cabinets misread the specifications of the original cabinets. Naturally, my wife and I would like to have the cabinets conform to the standard of their predecessors with as little delay as possible, and we will appreciate hearing from you as to when this will be effected.

Yours sincerely,

Wade Orflote

c.c. Ahmad Mann, Cloke & Dagah Construction Ltd.

A copy would also have been sent to the broker had you purchased the policy through an agent, but since you have always dealt with the insurance company directly, only one copy is sent, to the contractor.

The terminology is firm, but complimentary when deserved to dispel any suspicion that you may be a professional complainer, and you have not made reference to any disagreement with Messrs. Gant and Mann. This will give all parties an opportunity to correct the installation without loss of face if called to task by the president. You mentioned the scratched cabinets but made no accusations. The cabinet manufacturer can now be held responsible, which will allow the installers to maintain their status in the eyes of the president and permit them to capitulate to your advantage.

Expressing yourself in a positive manner can help to tip the balance. Try to reduce the amount of thinking the recipient of your letter has to do, particularly if the thinking might not go in your favor. Notice that the penultimate sentence to Ms. Penny Wise concludes, "hearing from you as to when this will be effected," as opposed to "might" or "could." A minor point, but details are important.

If this letter fails to produce results, then you will have to be more forceful. But before writing your next ultimatum, obtain a couple of quotes from reputable cabinetmakers for duplicating your original cabinets. Make sure the quotes include taxes and installation. Then send another letter, to the chairman this time. No harm in letting him know what you think of his president. Send a copy to the president in any case, so she won't be missing anything.

45 Perrel Avenue
Gullibal
D3G 6Q2

Pulla, Faastwun Insurance Inc.
Ethix-Notus Towers
Pirana
B3N 8M7

October 29, 1991

For the attention of Glen Fiddich, Chairman

Dear Mr. Fiddich,

My correspondence with your president, Ms. Penny Wise,
concerning my claim #75531/RT, appears to be causing
some confusion.

Accordingly, I have been obliged to obtain a separate
quotation to have the work successfully completed by a
reputable cabinetmaker, which I enclose for your
approval. Before I authorize Mr. Logplane's company to
go ahead, I thought it best to check with you first, in case
you prefer to pay him direct, rather than remit to me
upon completion of the job.

I look forward to your immediate remittance, and
instructions.

Yours sincerely,

Wade Orflote

c.c. Penny Wise, President
    Ahmad Mann, Cloke & Dagah Construction Ltd

This letter is a little presumptuous and just a shade on the cheeky side, but it
does give the impression that you are moving ahead with unstoppable determination. The chances are that it will swing the balance. Besides, the chair-

man might find your audacity so breathtaking that he authorizes payment out of sheer admiration!

If he doesn't, then the final option should be sent as follows:

---

45 Perrel Avenue
Gullibal
D3G 6Q2

Pulla, Faastwun Insurance Inc.
Ethix-Notus Towers
Pirana
B3N 8M7

November 7, 1991

For the attention of Glen Fiddich, Chairman

Dear Mr. Fiddich,

I am in receipt of your letter of November 5, and note that your company is not prepared to take the necessary steps to correct the faulty workmanship in my home perpetrated by a contractor selected and appointed by you, in settlement of claim #75531/RT.

Unless the repairs are satisfactorily completed, or I receive a check for $2,783.98 as per the quotation by Mr. S. Bruce Logplane, by Monday, November 25, 1991, a court summons will be filed without further notice.

Yours sincerely,

Wade Orflote

c.c. Penny Wise, President
     Ahmad Mann, Cloke & Dagah Construction Ltd.
     Yasser Nosur, Federal Insurance Bureau

As in the previous section about property damage not covered, a separate letter enclosing the correspondence thus far can be sent to the Federal Insurance Bureau, with copies of *that* letter sent to Mr. Fiddich, Ms. Wise, and Mr. Mann.

This really should be enough to convince the insurers that they ought to comply with your wishes. In the unlikely event that they are still reluctant, the summons is the next step in the proceedings.

SETTLEMENT FOLLOWING AN ACCIDENT

Insurance is merely a sophisticated version of gambling, with the odds stacked against the customer. When you insure your car, you are in effect betting the insurer that you are not going to have an accident within a certain time period. Unfortunately, it is the insurer who determines the amount of the bet, or premium, and who keeps the stake even when you win! If you win, you might get a small discount on next year's premium. If you lose, the insurer will be anxious to keep as much of the stake as possible by settling your claim for the lowest possible price.

Insurance companies appoint adjusters, who look at a damaged vehicle and submit an "independent" evaluation of the cost of repairs. If you disagree with the assessment, the insurance company will be quick to assure you that the firm doing the evaluation is entirely independent, completely unbiased, and not subject to any pressure or commercial loyalty. This claim is of course absolute nonsense!

Adjusters do operate independently, with no direct affiliation to any insurance company. But since they are appointed by the insurer, and not the insured, they are clearly working for the insurance company. They are, in fact, subcontractors who must comply with the instructions and business principles dictated by the insurance company that pays them.

Insurance adjusters prey on the sense of guilt almost everyone involved in an automobile accident feels. Whether an accident is your fault or not, you will feel guilty about vehicle damage or injuries, guilty when you explain what happened to a uniformed officer in front of the mob of spectators that meets regularly at all traffic accidents, guilty when you have to confess to your insurance company or broker that you have betrayed their faith in you, and guilty when you face the estimator. Assuming the insured will be grateful to accept any reasonable settlement, the insurer will dictate the most expedient and cheapest terms.

The purpose of insurance is to provide the funds to replace lost or damaged goods, or to restore them to the condition they were in at the time of loss or damage. This includes automobile insurance, although anyone who has made a claim must think that it is subject to a completely different set of rules. Following an automobile accident, the insured will usually accept a percentage of the actual loss in compensation with only minimal protest.

The numerous ploys the insurer practices on the unwary victim are varied and profitable. If the car is still drivable, you will be asked to take the damaged vehicle to a body shop specified by the insurers and at their convenience. If the car is not drivable, it will be towed to the preferred shop by the insurer. Any request that the vehicle be taken to a shop of your choosing is dismissed, and you are told that unless you comply with their instructions, the claim will be impossible to process. Insurers and adjusters may use body shops that will install substitute or used parts in order to keep costs at a minimum. In addition, some body shops will supplement an adjuster's salary to ensure a continuing flow of wrecks. Small wonder, therefore, that your request for the repairs to be made at the shop of your choice is not well received!

Cooperate with the insurers, but then take your car to a body shop of your choice for an independent estimate. If you prefer your shop to do the repairs, you should notify the insurance company of your decision, authorize the repair, and the insurers will have to meet the bill no matter how much they protest.

You may, on the other hand, decide you prefer to fix it yourself and receive a check for the estimated amount. Invariably the insurers will tell you that they can only pay the body shop after the job is completed, and that if you insist on cash, they will only offer a percentage of the total amount. This is illegal; they have to pay the full amount whether the car is repaired or not. Not only do they have to settle in full with you, as opposed to paying whoever completes the job, but their payment must be based on the estimate from the body shop you would have chosen had you elected to have the work done regardless of price or any other factor not to their liking. Even if you decide to have the car repaired, they are still obliged to settle with you, and not the body shop.

You can do what you like with your car, no matter what terms are erroneously dictated to you. If you want to leave the car with a few dents and spend the money on a trip to Disneyland, there is absolutely nothing the insurers can do about it. Their contract with you is merely to ensure that you are reimbursed for any damage to your car, and not to supervise or enforce how the money is used after it has been paid to you.

If the estimate exceeds or is close to the present value of the vehicle, let's say $2,000, with damage costing $2,500, the insurers will tell you that they have decided to cut their losses by writing the car off. Which means that without consulting you, they are going to scrap your car, and you are probably going to be offered a settlement as far below its real value as they can persuade you to accept. Alternatively, they might provide you with their interpretation of an equivalent vehicle. You are under no obligation to accept either of these offers. The car is your property, and you are perfectly within your rights to insist on the amount needed to repair it. Damage is damage, and has to be paid for, no matter what the value of the injured vehicle. If the car had been worth $20,000.00, they would have let you keep it, and repaired it. There is no reason why they should be allowed to save at least $500 because of your impecunious circumstances!

If you are deprived of the use of your vehicle in an accident through the fault of a third party, then in addition to making sure that you claim the full amount of the repair at your preferred shop, you are entitled to the use of a rental car until the work is completed. Make certain you use one of the major rental companies even though they will be expensive, after all you wouldn't want to risk another accident by renting an old wreck from a bargain-basement agency! You have been rudely and blamelessly separated from your own transportation, and the responsible party or their insurers must include a temporary substitute in the settlement. Here again, the adjusters will invariably deny responsibility. If your car is used only for pleasure, they will insist that you would only be entitled to a substitute for business use. But in fact, what you use the car for is irrelevant — if you are no longer able to use it, they are responsible for any and all costs relating to this loss. If the accident is partially or wholly your fault, or if you are making a claim on your own insurance, then you may or may not be entitled to a rental car. Check your policy.

In the event you don't exercise your option to rent a car, and prefer to pocket the money that would have been spent on the rental, obtain a detailed quote from the rental agency, including mileage charges, taxes, etc., and add this to the amount you will be claiming from the insurers, together with the estimate for the damaged vehicle and any other losses caused by the accident, such as excessive time off work if the adjusters do not meet you at the appointed time, secondary damage to goods in the car at the time of the accident, and any injury or loss suffered by your passengers.

If you or a passenger is physically injured, you will almost certainly wish to consult a lawyer. If you do appoint a lawyer (see chapter 10), you may still wish to settle the claim for the damaged vehicle yourself so that you can quickly effect repairs or purchase a replacement. Otherwise, ask your lawyer to make the vehicle claim separately and as soon as possible.

One fine day, you are driving home and are confronted by a red traffic signal. You obey the light, but as you sit innocently in your stationary conveyance, you hear the screech of tires behind you, followed by the sound and feel of metal on metal. You find you and your car pushed unwillingly down the road. Luckily you are not hurt. You alight from your car to inspect the damage and make the acquaintance of your assailant.

The damage to the back of your car is extensive, but the other driver appears uninjured. You leave the cars where they are and call the police. It is particularly important not to move either vehicle, even if it means creating a massive traffic jam, for their position will determine who is liable for the incident. While you wait for the police, you exchange insurance details, names, addresses, and telephone numbers. The officer takes both your statements, awards a ticket for careless driving to your new friend, and then, after making sure your car is still safe enough to drive, you continue on your journey. Before doing so, however, note the name, number, and station telephone number of the attending officer, just in case you need to clarify any details of your claim. For the same reason, jot down the names, addresses, and telephone numbers of any witnesses.

Since you are clearly blameless in this case, you will be claiming all damages from the insurer of the vehicle that hit you. You call that company as soon as possible and make an appointment to have an adjuster verify the damage. There is no need to involve your own company or broker; you can conduct the claim yourself. However, it is a good idea to let your insurers know what has happened, making it clear that the other party is entirely liable — otherwise your accident and claim record may be blemished. Tell them you will be negotiating the settlement without their assistance.

Before you take the car to the body shop specified by your assailant's insurers, take it to two other shops for estimates. One should be owned by a dealership specializing in selling and maintaining your make of vehicle. They will be familiar with your car, will be better able to judge any hidden damage to your make, and will probably base their estimate on new factory parts. A shop supervised by the adjuster may use secondhand parts, body filler, and "clone" body parts made by unauthorized manufacturers. Don't forget to include the cost of a rental car in the estimates.

Armed with your two estimates, you arrive at the shop appointed by the adjuster. He examines the damage with the shop's estimater, and after much discussion between the two, out of earshot, he prepares his estimate.

Meanwhile, you assess the appearance of the shop. Your initial inspection does not inspire confidence. The floor is filthy and cluttered with bits of twisted metal and trim. The mechanics are wearing extremely dirty overalls. At the back of the shop, a car is being painted with no protection from the considerable dust in the shop. You are not impressed. In fact, you are concerned about the quality of the repairs — shoddy repairs will be visible to the experienced eye of a dealer and will reduce the value of your car, should you wish to sell it.

You point out your misgivings to the adjuster. He assures you that these people will do an excellent job and that he regularly recommends the shop to several different insurance companies. His estimate is $1,376.00, and the repairs will take three days.

You now present your two alternative estimates. The quote from the independent shop is $1,684.00, plus car rental for three days at $25.00 per day, for a total of $1,759.00. The dealership's body shop quotes $1,743.00, with a four-day loan of a courtesy car for $40.00, totaling $1,783.00.

The adjuster immediately becomes defensive, and tells you that body shops are always more realistic when dealing with adjusters than with individuals, and that since the insurance company is paying for the repairs, it has the prerogative to appoint a particular shop for the job, which in this case is the one you are visiting. Besides which, the company will not pay for a rental car because you don't use your vehicle for business. He gives you an ultimatum: if you want the job done, you will have to adhere to the insurer's terms; if you fail to comply with this "normal" procedure, the claim will not be processed, and you will forfeit your right of settlement.

You now demonstrate that your naïveté has been somewhat overestimated. You know exactly how much you are entitled to settle for, and you have to convince him that your familiarity with the principles of automobile insurance is at least as good as his own. Calmly give notice that you have carefully considered the merits of the three estimates, and have decided that, without question, the dealership is best suited to make the most professional repair. To this end, you require a check for $1,783.00 in full settlement without delay.

If he argues that you cannot take your car to the most expensive shop, you tell him that you chose that particular quote entirely on merit and that since the damaged vehicle is owned by you, and not the insurance company, only you have the right to decide where it will be repaired. If you are offered a reduced amount unless the check is paid to a body shop, remind the adjuster that such a discount is illegal and that the insurer is obliged to pay the total amount of the claim, whether or not the repairs are made. Again you tell him that you own the car, and that it is up to you to decide how the settlement money is spent.

If he protests the rental car, point out that since the insurers are liable for all losses resulting from their client's negligence, deprivation of the use of your vehicle cannot be excluded from the claim. Furthermore, even though the car is still theoretically drivable, you are not prepared to risk another accident as a consequence of mechanical damage that may yet come to light when the vehicle is thoroughly checked during repairs. Besides which, you do not see why you should drive a damaged car when you are entitled to one in good condition. Therefore, you are going to drive to the dealership's body shop, leave the car for repairs, and rent a suitable replacement until a check for the full settlement is received. All storage charges, and the accumulating cost of the rental car will be invoiced to the insurer on a weekly basis until the claim is satisfactorily settled!

Inform the adjuster that as soon as you have left your disfigured conveyance at its destination and picked up your rental, you will be writing to his client Mr. Hugh Jacksedent, president of The Fought Knocks Insurance Corporation. Ask for the adjuster's business card, or if he doesn't have one, his employer's full name and address; the president will need to know who is responsible for the circumstances that have obliged you to write to him directly.

Unless this is the first day in his chosen profession, the adjuster will be fully aware that the compensation you have specified is legitimate, and that you have the knowledge and tenacity to enforce your claim. He may authorize a settlement on your terms or he may need to get permission "from above," which he can do by telephone from the shop.

Should you settle, ask the adjuster for the name and telephone number of the person who will be handling the settlement. You call that person as soon as you get home to make sure that the check will be for the full amount and to ask when you may expect to receive it. If the amount and date for remittance meet with your approval, then you need do nothing more than wait.

If the adjuster remains unconvinced by your steadfast insistence and refuses to comply with your wishes, inform him of your intended action and then take your car and leave. When you get home, call the dealership and ask them what they charge for storage, then call a car rental agency for their daily charge, including of course all mileage and tax surcharges.

You now write to the insurers, as follows:

---

55 Acacia Avenue
Unown City
P1K 3CV

The Fought Knocks Insurance Corporation
Cardent Building
Mammon
E2R 7J8

April 2, 1992

For the attention of Hugh Jacksedent, President

Dear Mr. Jacksedent,

Two days ago, on March 31, one of your clients, Mr. Kit Chinsink, holder of Policy No. 65983467348724 with your company, failed to observe that my car was stopped at a red traffic signal and drove into the rear end of my vehicle, causing considerable damage. The police confirmed that Mr. Chinsink was entirely liable for the collision. They also charged him with careless driving.

After the police concluded their report, I exchanged the necessary personal and vehicle details with your client, and later telephoned your offices to report the collision to a Mrs. Dinah Sorre. Mrs. Sorre instructed me to take my car to A. Salt & Vialants Auto Body, 546 Grime Street, at 1 p.m. today, where I would be met by your claim adjuster, Mr. Don Alduk from Mak-Arber Insurance Adjusters.

On the way to the stated body shop, I went to the trouble of obtaining two additional quotations for our mutual benefit, so that we might select the shop best suited to cope with this particular type of damage.

After Mr. Alduk had inspected the car and confirmed the extent of the required repairs, I discussed the matter with him in some detail. I expressed my lack of confidence in the work I had witnessed in progress at Messrs. A. Salt & Vialants. We then reviewed the two quotations I had obtained earlier in the day, and upon careful analysis and reflection, I decided that the estimate (enclosed) from Grumbal-Wiyne Blunderville Ltd. represented the best alternative. Their clean and efficient premises had impressed me, and the make of my car is a Blunderville, a model they specialize in.

To my astonishment, Mr. Alduk greeted my decision with an alarming battery of protests, none of which were valid, including the following:

- My car had to be repaired wherever Mr. Alduk dictated, irrespective of suitability or my preference.
- The claim had to be paid to the repairer on completion of the job, and not to the owner of the vehicle.
- A rental car would not be provided even though I would be deprived of my vehicle because of your client's negligence. You are legally obliged to provide

restitution equal to all damages resulting from any automobile accident.

- If I choose not to have the car repaired, or to have the work done at a later date, any cash settlement would only be a percentage of the total claim.

I can scarcely believe that a symbol of solid respectability like The Fought Knocks Insurance Corporation would knowingly risk its reputation by appointing a firm of adjusters so lamentably unaware of prevailing insurance legislation, and can only assume that you are unaware of the standards practiced by your representatives.

Please inform me that this disgraceful performance will be investigated immediately. Meanwhile I enclose my invoice for the accident for immediate and full settlement.

Please be aware that since professional opinion is that my damaged car is too dangerous to use, I am obliged to leave the vehicle with the proposed repairers and rent a replacement until I receive a check in full settlement. Storage charges are $25.00 per week, and car rental is $298.54 per week. These expenses will be invoiced to you every seven days until my claim is settled.

I look forward to your early response.

Yours sincerely,

Mary Dryver

Encls.

c.c. Mike Arzhurt, President, Insurance Bureau of Canada

The prospect of a regular weekly bill of $323.54, and a potential rap on the knuckles from the Insurance Bureau should elicit a quick and cooperative response.

Note that only one estimate, the one you selected, has been sent with your letter — there is no advantage to be gained by sending all three. Besides, if the president needs further information, he can contact the adjuster or you.

You also enclose a separate invoice, so that the president can send it down to the settlement department without delay. An invoice is resistant to adjustment and demands to be paid in total. It should include the cost of repairs, lost income, and other expenses. Although you may be annoyed by the attitude and principles demonstrated by the adjuster and insurer, your claim must be kept to a reasonable and legal level. If the insurer thinks that you are out to take them for a ride, they will be very uncooperative, and your negotiating credibility will be greatly diminished. Therefore, if your car is drivable and you continue to use it, you should not invoice for storage and rental charges.

It is unlikely that your letter and invoice will not be speedily settled, but if you have not received a check within about a week, a final demand is in order, as follows:

---

55 Acacia Avenue
Unown City
P1K 3CV

The Fought Knocks Insurance Corporation
Cardent Building
Mammon
E2R 7J8

April 10, 1992

For the attention of Don Tuargu, Chairman

Dear Mr. Tuargu,

My invoice for $1,830.65 dated April 2, sent for the attention of your president, Mr. Hugh Jacksedent, with a request for immediate settlement, appears to have escaped his attention.

I know you will be aware of your urgent legal liability concerning this matter, and trust that I may rely upon you to ensure that Mr. Jacksedent remits without delay.

Failure to do so by Monday, April 20, 1992, will
precipitate my filing a summons, without further notice.

I look forward to your prompt cooperation.

Yours sincerely,

Mary Dryver

c.c. Hugh Jacksedent, President
     Mike Arzhurt, President, Insurance Bureau of Canada

Since you have not sent the chairman any details of the claim you are asking
him to investigate, he will have to ascertain the urgency and content of the
case by contacting Mr. Jacksedent. The copies to the president and the Insurance Bureau should give Mr. Jacksedent further incentive to settle before em-
barrassing questions and investigations begin to encroach upon his usual daily
routine.

In the very remote likelihood that you meet with a negative response, then
a summons should be filed as soon as possible after the April 20 deadline
given in your letter. But even the most obstinate insurance company will realize the futility of contesting your justifiable claim, and you should soon receive your settlement.

5

Satisfaction Guaranteed: Taking on the Retailers

Most of us must deal with retailers almost daily, buying groceries, prescription drugs or glasses, clothing or footwear, and so on. Usually, such goods, if purchased from a reputable store, are sound. However, occasionally merchandise may be inferior or break down prematurely.

REFUSAL TO REFUND FOR FAULTY MERCHANDISE

In recent years, thanks in part to legislation, advances in communication — which speed the dissemination of bad publicity — and increased competition among manufacturers and retailers, it has become easier to obtain a refund for products that prove to be defective. Despite such encouraging signs of enlightenment, however, there will always be a few retailers who steadfastly refuse to take back faulty goods, even when a receipt is presented. On the other hand, customers who ask for refunds without receipts can try the patience of even the most willing and tolerant retailer; retailers can hardly be expected to remember selling merchandise to a customer six months ago, or refund money for merchandise that may have been purchased from another supplier.

Having said that, I am reminded of a friend's recent experience: her television cable converter died after two years of reliable service. The item was purchased with a one-year guarantee from a large chain of retailers, which will remain anonymous but whose name suggests that they operate north of the border and are committed to selling round black objects that surround wheel rims. . . . My friend took the deceased converter to the nearest outlet, without a receipt, and offered it to the returns clerk. The clerk gave it hardly a glance, said, "These often seem to come back," and promptly gave my friend a brand-new converter — a newer and better model than the original. So there is hope!

There are steps you can take to reduce the likelihood of your purchases failing prematurely: use the goods only for their intended purpose (for instance a cellular telephone may deteriorate rapidly if it's used while scuba-diving!); pay attention to special instructions or requirements. If you keep your receipts, use your purchases for the purpose intended, and do not treat them to any unrealistic excesses, you will have done all that is required to substantiate a claim if the goods fail to perform adequately or for as long as could reasonably be anticipated.

Let us assume that you purchased an expensive pair of high-heeled shoes to wear to the office. Since they were rather more than you could afford at the time, you look after them with more care than normal and only wear them in clement weather. One fine day ten weeks later, the local bus drivers are working to rule (which rule, and what dark secret it harbors, nobody knows), and thus you decide to walk to work, wearing The Shoes. As you step off the sidewalk at an intersection, there is a sharp noise from your right heel as it parts company with the rest of the shoe, and you feel yourself falling. Fortunately your descent is arrested by a fellow pedestrian. You hobble over to a nearby while-you-wait heel-and-sole store, where the shoemaker informs you that the shoes are so poorly made, he won't fix them! You have no choice but to proceed to the office barefoot.

After work, you pay a visit to the department store that sold you the footwear. You ask for the manager, who is in and willingly grants an audience. However, the manager's accommodating and obsequious manner swiftly deteriorates as, while examining the invalid shoes, she conducts an intensive interrogation about their use. You calmly answer all her questions and inform her that you have the receipt at home and can produce it the next day, if necessary. The manager informs you that since they are fashion shoes and not walking shoes, they have been subjected to far greater strain than they were designed to withstand, and that she can see nothing at all wrong with the workmanship. In fact the shoes are from a very reputable manufacturer, and this is the first time anyone has returned with a complaint. She refuses to accept liability even with the receipt. Aghast at such callous dismissal, you protest no further, and retreat complete with damaged shoes.

It is probably not practical for most footwear manufacturers to offer a guarantee for a specific length of time since some people go through shoes almost as quickly as most people use paper handkerchiefs. Having bought one pair of shoes, such people could conceivably have free replacements at the expense of the manufacturer for the rest of their lives! However, it is reasonable to expect a reputable retailer or manufacturer to judge individual complaints according to their merit.

Now it is time to address the matter in writing. You have a choice of seeking redress from either the retailer or the manufacturer, or both. In this case, you write to the retailer since they are responsible for selling you the shoes and offered no written or verbal warning that their life expectancy was two and a half months. Also, the customer's contract is with the retailer, not with agents or suppliers. If the customer successfully obtains a replacement or refund, it is up to the retailer to make appropriate arrangements with the supplier for credit. By all means, though, send a copy of the correspondence to the manufacturer.

The letter to the store could read as follows:

---

925 Tipe Avenue
Apartment 404
Shuless
H5D 3V6

Pathrew Thenoez Stores Inc.
100 Sezermy Street
Kutthrote
K9F 5P3

October 25, 1991

For the attention of Howie Kondme, President

Dear Mr. Kondme,

On August 21, 1991, I purchased from your store on Main Boulevard, Shuless, a pair of Bunyan Akes shoes, for the price of $197.99 (photocopy of receipt enclosed).

I particularly chose Bunyan Akes, as they have a good reputation and their advertising always strongly suggests that their products are well made and comfortable. I elected to make my investment at one of your stores, since I have been a customer for many years, you always have a good selection of merchandise, and I always receive quick and courteous service.

I was thoroughly distressed, therefore, when, while I was strolling to work, a heel snapped right off one of my new shoes as I was crossing a busy intersection. Although shaken, I was fortunately not injured, and took the shoes to a nearby shoe repairer to see what could be done. The shoemaker refused to repair the shoes because they were of such poor quality!

I took the shoes back to your store that evening, where I was told by your footwear department manager, Ms. Anne Olbute, that the break was caused by excessive walking! I am sure that you will agree that Ms Olbute's analysis is, to say the least, less than accurate; I have rarely worn the shoes in the short time since buying them, as can be verified by the lack of wear on the soles and heels, and have never worn them in the rain or snow.

There must, therefore, be a fault in the design or manufacturing process of which I am an innocent victim, and I will be most grateful to receive your authorization of a complete refund of the purchase price.

No doubt you will require the shoes so that you can send them back to Bunyan Akes, and I will be pleased to leave them at your store when I collect my refund.

I would appreciate your settling this matter at your earliest convenience.

Yours sincerely,

Tanya Hyde

c.c. U.C. Clogg, President, Bunyan Akes Footwear Inc.

In your letter you have stressed that you are a regular and normally appreciative customer, that possible physical injury was narrowly avoided, and that the goods do not live up to the standards claimed in advertisements. You have refrained from suggesting any deliberate malpractice by the store. At the same time, you are concerned by the department manager's reaction, which must be redressed if the store is to retain a loyal customer.

If the store refuses to comply with your wishes, then another letter should be sent as follows:

925 Tipe Avenue
Apartment 404
Shuless
H5D 3V6

Pathrew Thenoez Stores Inc
100 Sezermy Street
Kutthrote
K9F 5P3

October 29, 1991

For the attention of Howie Kondme, President

Dear Mr. Kondme,

I have read your letter of October 28, and I am
astonished to learn that you are not prepared to
authorize the refund to which I am clearly entitled.

I find it difficult to believe that an organization the size of
Pathrew Thenoez Stores does not employ anyone with
sufficient technical knowledge to recognize a sincere and
valid claim initiated by the poor workmanship in goods sold.

Unless the amount claimed, $197.99, is settled in full by
Tuesday, November 12, 1991, a court summons will be
filed without further notice. The damaged shoes will be
produced as evidence at the trial.

Yours sincerely,

Tanya Hyde

c.c. U.C. Clogg, President, Bunyan Akes Footwear Inc.
Wun Hung Lo, President, Retail Council Federation

There may be various retail associations and possibly government-sponsored
consumer-protection agencies who act as watchdogs for the consumer. Your
local library or community center should be able to track them down.

When you send copies to these agencies, include all previous correspondence so that they will have all the facts. The more associations the merrier; the store probably wouldn't want its reputation brought to their attention. This second and final letter, with its copies going to appropriate regulatory bodies, should certainly encourage the store to suddenly see your point of view in a more accommodating light, and a refund should be on its way with little delay. Otherwise you will have to proceed to small claims court.

MERCHANDISE BREAKS DOWN AFTER WARRANTY EXPIRES

Have you ever wondered why some goods seem to have an internal clock that starts ticking as soon as you make your purchase, and then expires immediately after the guarantee has done likewise? How often your purchase is used makes no difference. The guarantee runs out on Tuesday, and the item dies in sympathy on Wednesday.

Returning the goods to the vendor and pleading that the warranty be honored as it is only a day or two on the wrong side of the expiry date usually proves to be an exercise in futility. You will invariably be told that if the manufacturer had intended to supply a guarantee of 366 days, this would have been printed on the warranty. Therefore, at one second after midnight following the day of expiry, you are entirely responsible for the expense of repairing or replacing the faulty goods.

With few exceptions, most customers will assume their rights are indeed limited to the conditions imposed by the manufacturer, and after a brief attempt to obtain a sympathetic extension, they give up. This is good news for the manufacturers; they save a great deal of money by not having to replace faulty goods, and their profits soar when customers have to purchase a replacement. Unscrupulous manufacturers even reduce the quality of their goods to last only as long as the warranty. Such manufacturers may risk losing customers to competitors, but the overall increase in business usually outweighs any losses.

Most warranties cover the minimum period that manufacturers can comfortably get away with, and may include all manner of escape clauses, such as excluding labor, shipping costs to the factory, damage to user or property as a consequence of failure of the goods, and so forth. But if a long warranty is unreasonable to a manufacturer, a short one is unfair to the customer. Before you purchase any item, you should do a little homework to find out what the probable life expectancy of your potential purchase is. Check with a couple of reputable firms who specialize in repairs to the type of item you are intending to buy.

Let's suppose you recently bought a vacuum cleaner, which has broken down after twelve months and one day. You take it back to the store where it was purchased, and you are told that the motor has burned out and needs to be replaced. The bad news is that the warranty expired at the end of twelve months, so you will have to pay for the repair. The good news is that the new motor will come with a three-month warranty!

You protest that you have used the machine carefully, but to no avail, and you elect to leave with the machine unrepaired. When you get home, you call two alternative repairers, describe the problem, and ask them if a burned-out motor is a typical fault of this particular model. You are told that it is, and that you can expect the new one not to last more than a few months. In addition, the two repair shops confirm that three years would be a reasonable life expectancy for a vacuum cleaner like yours.

You now call the manufacturer of your recalcitrant machine, and ask for the service manager. Make sure you get his name before you speak to him. You will be making notes of the conversation, which may be used as evidence against the company later on. You tell him that you would like his expert opinion on a machine, made by his firm, that you are considering purchasing. Explain that your principal concern is reliability, and his opinion will be of great assistance in helping you decide whether the model in question is suited to your requirements.

You are pleased to be inundated with glowing testimony about the unparalleled performance and reliability of the marvelous machine, while your own defunct example sits forlornly on the floor. He assures you that it should be entirely problem-free for a good five years and that he personally knows of several that have been running like clockwork for much longer. You thank him kindly for his valuable and generous advice, and assure him that his firm will now enjoy the benefit of your immediate attention thanks in no small part to his very persuasive convictions!

But before expressing your grievance in writing, you must decide whether you want your money refunded or the vacuum cleaner repaired. The manufacturer will almost certainly prefer to repair the machine, which will be cheaper than refunding your money. Since you like the machine anyway, you decide to keep it.

Should you seek redress from the retailer or the manufacturer? In theory, the first approach in writing should be made to the retailers — you gave them your money in good faith and it is their responsibility to maintain customer satisfaction. In this case, however, a guarantee is the bone of contention and the retailers probably won't make repairs because they won't be reimbursed by the manufacturer. A letter to the manufacturer is in order, then, as follows:

22 Spotlis Avenue
Sweaping Mounds
G6H 8C3

Gryme Sucker Appliances Ltd.
Gleaming Towers
Nophilthe
Y7S 3P2

October 29, 1991

For the attention of Neal Toscrubb, President

Dear Mr. Toscrubb,

I am the owner of a Muk Maniak vacuum cleaner,
manufactured by your company, and purchased from Oarful
Appliances, 274 Fuzebloane Street, Sweaping Mounds.

This is an excellent machine in all respects, and I really
appreciate its light weight, powerful suction, and
unusually quiet operation, which allows me to hear the
telephone or doorbell while I am vacuuming.

Unfortunately, during routine use two days ago, my Muk
Maniak abruptly stopped, for no apparent reason, and I
took it back to the store. The machine was examined by
the manager, Mr. Oarful, who informed me the motor had
burned out and would have to be replaced.

I expressed surprise at this diagnosis since it was the
much advertised reputation for trouble-free operation
that convinced me to replace my old vacuum with a
Gryme Sucker. I received a further shock when Mr.
Oarful refused to repair my machine under warranty,
even though it is only just over twelve months old.
Apparently the guarantee is valid for only twelve
months, and he is not able to authorize repairs past that
time, even when the defect has occurred through no
fault of the user.

I checked the model's service reputation with a number of other repair shops, and I was most interested to learn that the motors on this model are prone to burning out prematurely and that even the replacements are subject to the same fate! Yet, curiously enough, when I called your factory to seek the opinion of your service manager, Mr. Li Ing, he expressed his enthusiasm and confidence in the Muk Maniak, and assured me that it "should be entirely problem-free for a good five years" and that he knows of many that have lasted for considerably longer.

Confusing, isn't it?

I am sure you will agree that a well-built vacuum cleaner merits a warranty that accurately reflects the confidence the makers have in its workmanship, and I cannot believe that your company expects the model in question to start giving trouble after only twelve months.

I look forward to your confirmation that my vacuum cleaner will be repaired under warranty at once, with no cost to me.

Yours sincerely,

Bess Tufikxit

c.c. U.R. Oarful, Manager, Oarful Appliances

The message should be abundantly clear. You have done your homework and discovered that Gryme Sucker machines are dropping like flies throughout the land while the company's service manager continues to sing their praises with no concern for reality. Mr. Toscrubb should antici-pate the possible adverse publicity if he does not act quickly to placate you. But, alas, he is not swayed by your flattery and diligence, and refuses to provide you with a new and trouble-free motor. You now write him another helpful letter, as follows:

22 Spotlis Avenue
Sweaping Mounds
G6H 8C3

Gryme Sucker Appliances Ltd.
Gleaming Towers
Nophilthe
Y7S 3P2

November 6, 1991

For the attention of Neal Toscrubb, President

Dear Mr. Toscrubb,

I was very surprised to receive your letter of November
4, which fails to adequately address my problem with a
vacuum cleaner made by your company.

I find it extraordinary to learn that a large company with
a reputation for quality and fair trading like yours is now
making goods that are totally inadequate for their
intended use. And furthermore, you refuse to provide
service facilities to correct the breakdowns that occur as
a result of these inadequacies.

Unless I receive written authorization for my machine to
be repaired free of charge, along with an extended
warranty for three years from the date of purchase, by
November 13, 1991, I will have the cleaner repaired and
invoice you for the full amount, plus my incurred
expenses. Should your company not settle the invoice, I
will not hesitate to file a court summons.

Yours sincerely,

Bess Tufikxit

c.c. U.R Oarful, Manager, Oarful Appliances
     Eve R. Kareful, President, Retail Council Federation

In the unlikely event that your wishes are still not being taken seriously, have the cleaner repaired, and send your invoice to the manufacturer, as promised. There is no need to include another letter with it.

Bess Tufikxit
22 Spotlis Avenue
Sweaping Mounds
G6H 8C3

Gryme Sucker Appliances Ltd
Gleaming Towers
Nophilthe
Y7S 3P2

November 18, 1991

For the attention of Neal Toscrubb, President

INVOICE #687/91

For replacement of prematurely failed motor to Muk Maniak vacuum cleaner, by Oarful Appliances on November 15, 1991	$137.58
Expenses (visits to repair shop, postage, etc.)	105.00
Total	$242.58

Terms: Payment by return. Overdue accounts attract interest at 1.5% per month.

UNLESS THIS ACCOUNT IS SETTLED IN FULL BY MONDAY DECEMBER 2, 1991, A COURT SUMMONS WILL BE FILED WITHOUT FURTHER NOTICE.

An invoice demands attention, and your persistence will show that you are unstoppable, which should produce a check.

The expenses may or may not be remitted, but if they are not, then further attempts to collect them are probably inadvisable.

6

Battles on the Home Front: Repairs and Renovations

A home, no matter how sweet, will need repairs from time to time. It would be prudent to keep a list of reliable trades — electrician, roofer, appliance repairer, and plumber — close to your phone as you would other emergency numbers.

DEFICIENT HOME RENOVATION

Building an addition or remodeling a home can involve considerable expense and inconvenience. Most homeowners are at the mercy of suppliers, contractors, designers, and architects, and can find their tempers sorely tried by the mess, disruption, and constant presence of strangers in their home.

Something can go wrong at any stage, delaying completion and adding further to the expense, even with a good contractor at the helm. Clearly prevention is better than cure. To this end, selecting a good architect or designer and a competent and honest contractor is essential. A recommendation from a trustworthy friend, neighbor, or professional organization is the best way to find both a contractor and an architect. Your local building inspectors may be able to provide you with a list of reliable contractors.

Meet with several architects, and discuss what you want built. You should have a budget in mind, and be clear about how architects establish their fees and how much the necessary drawings for your job will cost. Ask to see pictures of past projects, and check references. The architect you choose will prepare conceptual drawings from which you will select a design. After approving the final drawings, ask your architect to obtain quotes from at least three contractors. This will give you an opportunity to meet the three bidders and discuss the project with them.

If you are proceeding without an architect, you should also get quotes from three contractors. Make sure they are licensed with your local authority, and then invite them to the site. Beware of contractors who arrive at a price too quickly, particularly if the job is large or complex. A contractor who can start work immediately could also be doubtful: his ready availability may mean there is little demand for his type of workmanship. And beware of contractors who want a large deposit — they could be fly-by-night operators.

When assessing bids, don't necessarily accept the lowest, particularly if it is way below the next competitor's quote. The bidder may be using poor materials and unsuitable shortcuts, may have missed an important detail of the specification, or he may be deliberately bidding low to secure the project and will bill you for the "extras" later.

Once you have selected a contractor, you will want to discuss any possible problems, starting and completion dates, and a payment schedule before signing the contracts. As a general rule, the payments should always favor you, the customer. Apart from any legal entitlement to holdback on each payment made, you should not pay more than about two-thirds of the percentage of work completed. You will then always be comfortably in credit in the event the builder or one of his subcontractors defaults. Make sure you have a fixed price contract: a cost-plus arrangement might continue to cost and plus for much longer than you bargained for! Many local building authorities have useful, free booklets that cover the pitfalls of renovating and building.

When you begin building, be prepared for some disruption and inconvenience. Your contractor is your colleague; if you have complaints, discuss them with him calmly and away from his employees and subcontractors. If you are pleased with the work, draw his attention to it, preferably within earshot of the employees who actually did it! A few well-placed, sincere compliments will go far to soften hostilities should a dispute arise.

Should you have any new ideas or changes, you should discuss them with the contractor, not the subtrade involved. It is the contractor who is responsible for supervising all the trades on the job, and he has to know exactly what they are doing to maintain efficient coordination. Asking the heating contractor to move a duct over may seem a minor request, but it may be difficult for the plumber to route his pipes around it.

By all means offer the crew refreshments from time to time. But under no circumstances offer beer or any alcoholic beverages; your liability could be brought into question in the event of a subsequent injury or damage to property, no matter how little liquor was actually offered or consumed. And while good relations with those who are working on the job is no bad thing, don't spend so much time talking to employees that you distract them from their work. Most are paid on an hourly basis, and your contractor will be keen to see that his dollars are spent on productivity, not conversational dexterity.

Be prepared for unanticipated problems, and make sure you know the difference between an extra and work that should have been anticipated in the estimates. If framing behind a wall is found to be rotten, then replacing it is clearly an unanticipated, or extra, expense. On the other hand, plaster repairs to a wall after new plumbing is installed are predictable and should have been included in the original price. Make sure any alterations to the contract or extras are agreed to in writing, including the exact cost, no matter how small. Extras can add up, and unless they are kept strictly on record, the increased costs can be surprisingly high.

A contractor can be affected by events beyond his control — strikes, material shortages, and so on. Expect everything to take longer than anticipated, and plan accordingly. And if you spot something that is below standard or that has not been carried out according to the plans, bring it to the contractor's attention at once. The longer you delay, the more difficult and expensive it will become to make corrections. For example, it is easy to move a bathroom vanity before the fixtures are installed, but difficult and time-consuming once the tiles and fixtures are in.

Despite all precautions, however, disputes do occur. Should you become involved in a disagreement with your contractor, try to compromise. If you cannot arrive at an acceptable compromise by yourselves, agree to binding arbitration by your architect, if you have one, or another knowledgeable consultant. In some cases the building inspector can be called in, especially if the dispute concerns workmanship in his jurisdiction. It is important to find a quick and amicable solution, so that work can proceed without undue interruption.

Let us assume that you have just survived a major kitchen renovation, which was finished several days ago, and you have now spotted some irritating and potentially expensive deficiencies: one of the countertops has some chips and scratches that were touched up with paint, which has now worn off; some of the new ceramic tiles have come loose; and the subfloor squeaks. If you are using an architect or other qualified independent adviser, seek their opinion as to the validity of your complaint.

You call the contractor to ascertain his willingness to correct the problems, and after several failed attempts to locate him, and no effort on his part to return your calls, you are obliged to put your grievances in writing, as follows:

78 Daybree Crescent
Hacienda
D6S 4J3

Deral Liction Construction Ltd.
211 Ivasive Lane
Hacienda
D9K 3X2

March 1, 1992

For the attention of Lee Kinapype, President

Dear Lee,

You will be pleased to learn that I am very happy with our new kitchen.

Before you present your final account for payment, however, I should be most grateful if you could drop by to give me your valuable opinion on a couple of defects that appear to be in need of correction: the countertop on the north wall has some chips and scratches, and some of the tiles by the back entrance door have come loose, possibly because the floor in that area creaks slightly. I am sure the occasional flaw can occur in any major renovation, but we would not like your otherwise excellent workmanship to be marred by uncorrected problems.

I did call you a few times last week to let you know what had happened, but I daresay you have been very busy and unable to return my calls. Please call me as soon as possible to let me know when it will be convenient for you to inspect the countertop and ceramic floor.

I look forward to hearing from you.

Yours sincerely,

Luke Athemess

Since you were on first-name terms with the contractor, there is no reason why you should not continue to be so. You are trying to be as pleasant as possible in order to persuade him to bring the job up to his high standards, as well as your own, and the first communication should be phrased in suitably amicable expectation.

If you do not hear from him within three days, you may call to inquire if your letter has been received. If there is still no response, a further letter should be sent, as follows:

---

78 Daybree Crescent
Hacienda
D6S 4J3

Deral Liction Construction Ltd.
211 Ivasive Lane
Hacienda
D9K 3X2

March 7, 1992

For the attention of Lee Kinapype, President

Dear Lee,

Further to my earlier telephone calls, letter of March 1, and message left two days ago, your immediate response is now urgently requested.

Aside from the cosmetic and structural concerns that I have outlined, I am worried that the loose tiles could result in personal injuries, particularly to young children playing in the kitchen. The consequences of an accident do not bear thinking about, and I know you will share my anxiety that all preventive measures be taken without delay.

Kindly respond at your earliest.

Yours sincerely,

Luke Athemess

Deliver the letter by hand, if convenient, and mail a copy as well. This will ensure that he receives it, and will emphasize the degree of urgency and insistence that you are trying to convey. The prospect of a lawsuit for personal injury will serve as a powerful incentive to respond, and the unmistakable tone of your correspondence, together with his awareness that the final bill has yet to be settled, should produce a quick result.

And it does. The next day Mr. Kinapype calls to say he will be over later that evening to take a look at the alleged deficiency. He arrives as promised, but he protests liability for the countertop on the grounds that it has now been used for two weeks; he implies that the scratches and chips have been inflicted through domestic carelessness. Furthermore, he refuses to accept responsibility for the loose tiles; he accuses the occupants of the house of subjecting them to heavy traffic and abuse while they were still in the process of setting. You point out the paint touch-ups in the scratched countertop, but an explanation is not forthcoming, and he insists it was in perfect shape when installed, and was still so on completion of the job.

You assure him that no one went near the new tiles for three days after they were installed, and you demonstrate that the subfloor creaks; but he continues to insist that a minor creak would have no effect on the adherence of the tiles, and that they must have been subject to some abuse.

The discussion leads nowhere, and you are told that nothing can be done until the bill, which he has with him and presents to you, has been paid. As soon as the account is settled, he adds, any repairs can be made, but he is not liable for them, and they will have to be paid for just like any other job. Naturally, you do not pay the balance owing on his invoice, but without allowing the discussion to develop into an unpleasant argument, you invite him to leave, and let him know he will be hearing from you very shortly. Fortunately, the amount you still owe him is considerably more than the repairs would cost, but you still have to arrange for the work to be done, and if possible, conclude matters without too much trouble or delay.

It will be in your interest to prevent your relationship with the contractor from becoming irrevocably hostile — you may need to call him back in the future. Another letter is therefore in order.

78 Daybree Crescent
Hacienda
D6S 4J3

Deral Liction Construction Ltd.
211 Ivasive Lane
Hacienda
D9K 3X2

March 9, 1992

For the attention of Lee Kinapype, President

Dear Lee,

Further to our meeting last night, I am sorry that we could not arrive at a mutually agreeable solution to the countertop and tile problems discussed. You have my absolute assurance that none of my family damaged the countertop in question; the obvious paint touch-ups leave little doubt that the responsibility is not ours.

As for the loose tiles, I made quite sure that the floor was not walked upon or used in any way for three days after the tiles were installed. The tiles have loosened in an area that is not subject to heavy usage; therefore had we used the floor prematurely there would have been additional loose tiles where traffic is much heavier. It seems very likely, therefore, that the creaking subfloor is indeed the cause of the disturbance — an inflexible tile will not adhere properly to a flexible floor.

I realize that having to come back to remedy these problems is an annoyance, particularly since your suppliers or subcontractors are presumably responsible for the defects. However, I have great respect for your workmanship and integrity, and your cooperation in ensuring that the necessary repairs are completed without delay will be greatly appreciated.

The alternative, which is for me to hire another

contractor to do the work, is not an option I would willingly choose, as I am anxious to settle the balance of your invoice in full. I am unable to do so until the matter is resolved, preferably by your company, and I know you would not want to incur the expense of a competitor having to come and complete your otherwise excellent renovation.

Please let me know that you will be able to do the required work without delay.

Yours sincerely,

Luke Athemess

This should bring the desired response. In the unlikely event that he still refuses to cooperate, then you will have to obtain a couple of alternative quotes for the repairs, and send a final opportunity for him to comply with his obligations, as follows:

---

78 Daybree Crescent
Hacienda
D6S 4J3

Deral Liction Construction Ltd.
211 Ivasive Lane
Hacienda
D9K 3X2

March 12, 1992

For the attention of Lee Kinapype, President

Dear Lee,

I am sorry that you still feel unable to complete the necessary repairs to my kitchen, as described in my previous letters of March 1, 7, and 9.

I have consequently had to seek an alternative contractor to finish the job satisfactorily, and the firm I have

selected will do the work for the inclusive price of
$643.00, which I shall be obliged to deduct from my
check in settlement of your final account.

I still much prefer that you do the work, but unless you
let me know by March 16 that you are willing to do so, I
shall reluctantly proceed with the alternative quotation.

I trust that I may hear from you before March 16.

Yours sincerely,

Luke Athemess

If he does not comply with your last demand, have the work done by someone else, and deduct the amount from the final payment. That should conclude the matter. Most contractors will respond before their work is given to a rival, so protracted correspondence is not usually necessary. If you had been using an architect, you would, of course, have asked him or her to intervene on your behalf.

OVERCHARGE BY PLUMBER

Practically everyone has a horror story to tell about their experiences with a plumber. Ah, the much maligned plumber, struggling to earn an honest living in unsanitary conditions, often called out at unsocial hours, and yet he is seen as unpunctual, untidy, unreliable, and enormously wealthy through charging prices that might have made Al Capone consider a change of career!

Some plumbers are more reliable than others, just as some are more expensive than others. Inevitably, there are those who take advantage of a customer's predicament, especially when the job has to be done immediately. When you are presented with the bill, which will probably be more than you expected, how do you know whether you are being overcharged?

To alleviate any surprises, you should ask for an estimate first. A plumber may be reluctant to commit himself, but if his estimate is too high, and he refuses to negotiate, you have the option of sending him on his way and hiring another plumber. Of course, you risk a further delay and the next estimate might turn out to be even higher than the one you already have, and by the time you call the original plumber again, he may be out on another job and unable, or unwilling, to fit you into his new schedule.

Let's assume that one wet and windy night, you are woken by incessant barking from your dog. You plod angrily downstairs to offer advice to the unfaithful canine, who is sitting at the top of the basement stairs, but you are distracted by an unsavory odor. Vigorously brushing Fido aside, you switch on the basement lights to discover that the subterranean portion of your house is now several inches deep in a liquid that is definitely not pure rainwater! The source of the infiltration appears to be a floor drain, which would indicate a blockage somewhere outside the house.

Horror-struck, you sprint for the phone and call the emergency number for the city waterworks department. The bored clerk informs you that you must get a plumber to assess the problem. After a frenzied search in the yellow pages, you call a twenty-four-hour emergency service plumber that guarantees service within the hour. Sure enough, about fifty-five minutes after your call, two men arrive with various large items of equipment. They work in the rising waters for about three hours, and finally a shout of triumph precedes the welcome sight of water going down the drain. The plumbers inform you that the blockage was caused by debris that had collected in the pipe where it had been cracked by a tree root.

As they pack up their tools, you tremble with anticipation; you can hardly wait to see the bill. To your absolute horror, the invoice is even worse than expected — $980.00. You ask for a breakdown of the amount and are told that this is the standard charge for the job, and it includes a surcharge for working during the night and at short notice. The plumber is not keen to offer details of his hourly rate; he insists that this is not an excessive price for emergency work, and that no one has ever questioned it before. Besides, he does not set the rates, he just does the work, and is not allowed to leave the job site until it is paid.

So, how should you proceed? Fortunately, there are several factors in your favor, the most important being that you have achieved your objective, which was to have the blockage cleared quickly. Whatever happens, the probability of the blockage being reinstalled is reasonably remote! And payment is still in your hands, which is a definite advantage. It will be very difficult for the plumber to extract payment from you if the size of the bill cannot be satisfactorily explained, especially if you are willing to pay an amount you consider appropriate. (Partial payment demonstrates that you are willing to settle, provided the amount is reasonable, and also leaves a reduced amount outstanding, which may not be worth collecting. If you paid the full amount and tried to recover part of it later, you would probably have to resort to the courts.)

If the plumbers refuse to leave until they are paid, then you must inform them that they no longer have your permission to be on the premises, and therefore they are trespassing. If they insist on remaining against your instructions, warn them that you are going to call the police, particularly if they behave in a threatening manner. (If you must follow through, remember that disagreements over payments will be of no interest to the police because they are strictly a civil matter. So, when calling, refrain from describing the commercial aspect of the transaction. The police are only interested in upholding the law, and ensuring your personal safety.)

To encourage the plumbers to leave willingly, you tell them you have every intention of paying the bill, but not before it has been thoroughly analyzed by their boss — the proprietor or president. Get his full name, title, and telephone number, and what time he will be in his office. Ask the plumbers for their names and numbers as well. This will show them that you are serious about seeking a reduction and that you are not just looking for an excuse not to pay them. Eventually your strategy works, and they depart.

First thing in the morning, you call the proprietor to explain the situation and confirm your willingness to negotiate a fair price. If you write without calling first, the attending plumbers will have reported your nonpayment before your letter arrives, and the proprietor, not having heard from you, may assume an aggressive and fixed viewpoint, which will make your negotiations more difficult. Before you call, check with two or three alternative plumbers from the yellow pages, to see what they would have charged for the same job. If they are reluctant to say, you could mention that this has happened before and that you seem to recall it costing about $325.00 — or some other figure well below the amount of the invoice in dispute. This will precipitate a reaction, and will make it easy for them to give you a more accurate estimate. Once you have three estimates, make your call to the company that has just done the job.

You begin by complimenting the proprietor on his men's speedy response to your emergency and the short time it took them to locate and clear the blockage. This underlines the limited time the job took, reduces the justification for a large bill, and flatters his operation! Then, you inform him that you regret that you could not pay the bill in full as you are sure a mistake has occurred. You give him the three alternative quotes and stress that they are all for less than half the amount he has charged! You tell him you do not want to waste his valuable time in haggling, and are more than willing to pay him the amount of the highest of the three.

However, he becomes abusive, and you cut the conversation short, telling him you will let him know your intentions in writing. You do so in a letter like this:

56 Ouze Avenue
Poulinseler
Y3S 4R6

Brane Drain Ltd.
88 Block Street
Poulinseler
Y2H 2Q3

November 5, 1991

For the attention of Gord Elpus, President

Dear Mr. Elpus,

Further to our telephone conversation this morning concerning the blockage that was cleared by your workers earlier today, I confirm that I was pleased with the speed at which they turned out at short notice, and that the drain now seems to be working as it should.

Your invoice #3268, for the sum of $980.00 for the work, however, appears to have been computed erroneously since the job was completed in just over three hours. I discussed this alarming amount with your Mr. Sludje, who was in charge of the operation, but he was unable to help because the accounts are not under his control. I am therefore obliged to return the invoice for your attention, so that it can be corrected to a more realistic figure.

As a matter of interest, I checked with three of your competitors to see what they would have charged for the same job, and the quotes I was offered varied from $385.00 to $438.00. These prices are for their emergency service, and include taxes. Since you provided excellent service, which I would be pleased to recommend to anyone who may be unfortunate enough to suffer a similar emergency, I would be perfectly happy to settle your account at the highest of the three alternative quotes.

As soon as I am in receipt of your satisfactorily revised account, I will make full settlement by return mail.

Yours sincerely,

Ali Gayter

Encl.

No suggestion of gouging has been made. You are careful to avoid putting the company on the defensive, so that it will be easy for Mr. Elpus to explain away the overcharge as an accounting error.

You return the invoice with the letter; since you have no intention of paying it, there is no need to keep it. The ball is back in the company's court. But Mr. Elpus is unwilling to match the prices of his competitors, and returns his invoice with a demand for payment in full. You reply as follows:

---

56 Ouze Avenue
Poulinseler
Y3S 4R6

Brane Drain Ltd.
88 Block Street
Poulinseler
Y2H 2Q3

November 12, 1991

For the attention of Gord Elpus, President

Dear Mr. Elpus,

I have received your letter dated November 10, and the returned invoice #3268.

I find it completely unacceptable that you persist in charging me $980.00 for a total of seven man-hours' work! This is more than double the amount charged by the most expensive of your competitors, as I explained in my letter of November 5. I am perfectly willing to pay you a fair price for the job, and my offer to settle this matter by agreeing to match the most expensive figure quoted by your competitors is still valid. Anything in excess of this amount is out of the question. I therefore enclose a check for the sum of $438.00 in full and final settlement of your account.

Kindly issue a receipt, together with a credit for the erroneously charged balance, by return post.

Yours sincerely,

Ali Gayter

Encl.

c.c. Sybil Survent, Manager, Metro Licensing Authority
      Hon. Ian Kontinnent, Minister of Consumer Affairs

Your letter is firm and clear, and should convince him that this is absolutely all you are going to pay. Enclosing payment before the dispute has been settled is a calculated risk, with the odds in your favor. You have paid him at least the amount to which he is entitled, possibly more if the quote on which you based your payment is expensive. So you can be quite sure that the job was still very profitable, and that the proprietor does not have outstanding expenses from the work not covered by your check.

Had you decided not to pay anything at all, he would be justified in seeking redress through the courts. But you have established the prevailing rates, and paid accordingly, and he will realize that it will be difficult to get a favorable decision from any reasonable judge. Sending copies of the letter to the body that issues his business license, and the government agency responsible for retail and consumer guidelines and protection, should dampen his enthusiasm still further. So you are almost certainly safeguarded from any serious intent to pursue collection.

If there is further correspondence with the opposition, do not leave any communication unanswered. Failure to respond could be interpreted as an admission of liability by the courts, should you have the misfortune to need arbitration. A short reply to any further demands for payment could read as follows:

56 Ouze Avenue
Poulinseler
Y3S 4R6

Brane Drain Ltd.
88 Block Street
Poulinseler
Y2H 2Q3

November 18, 1991

For the attention of Gord Elpus, President

Dear Mr. Elpus,

I am in receipt of your letter dated November 16.

I regret that you do not appear to understand that the
sum of $438.00, which I remitted on November 12, is in
full and final payment of your account dated November 5.

Demands for further monies are completely unjustified,
and will not be met.

If you feel that the prospect of your using alternative
methods to pursue the matter will alter my position, I am
afraid you are very much mistaken.

Yours sincerely,

Ali Gayter

c.c. Sybil Survent, Manager, Metro Licensing Authority
    Hon. Ian Kontinnent, Minister of Consumer Affairs

This letter is brief and makes your position clear. You will notice that the
letter does not address any points that may have been raised by Mr. Elpus. You
are past the stage of discussion, and only wish to convey that you are tired of
his time wasting and futile persistence.

He may retain lawyers who send you a letter threatening action within a specified time. Such a letter is unlikely to result in the litigation threatened or implied, but will require a reply to call their bluff. Something like this usually works quite well:

---

56 Ouze Avenue
Poulinseler
Y3S 4R6

Thrett, Snarll, & Pounts, Solicitors
Charck Lane
Poulinseler
Y3R 2H7

November 28, 1991

Dear Sirs,

I received a letter dated November 24 from your Ms. Barb
E. D. Thrett, purportedly acting on behalf of Brane Drain Ltd.

If Ms. Thrett wishes me to elaborate on any points that
she may find confusing, I would be pleased to do so
before a judge, at her earliest convenience.

Yours sincerely,

Ali Gayter

c.c. Gord Elpus, Brane Drain Ltd.
     Sybil Survent, Manager, Metro Licensing Authority
     Hon. Ian Kontinnent, Minister of Consumer Affairs

No ambiguity in this one! Lawyers' letters don't scare me. If you want to sue, then go ahead.

You have deliberately departed from the practice of addressing mail to the principal. This shows that, although Ms. Thrett is clearly a senior partner in the firm, you are not impressed by either her credentials or her letter, and that by not addressing her directly you are not taking her very seriously. Your complete lack of concern will raise doubts as to the merit of pursuing the matter any further.

Once the matter has been settled to your satisfaction, you should check your status with the local credit bureau to ensure that you are not listed as a risk. Credit bureaus can attach information concerning a debt or unpaid account to a file without confirming the accuracy of the documentation, and unless details of any settlement or agreement are subsequently received, the risk status will not be reversed. If your file has been affected by the plumbing incident, then a meeting with someone at the bureau who can review your status in light of all the correspondence that transpired should restore your rating.

RENOVATOR PUTS UNJUSTIFIED LIEN ON HOUSE

Whenever you undertake major renovations to your property, you should make sure you are adequately protected against liens.

Basically, a lien is a right to assume possession of a property on which a debt is outstanding until the amount owed is discharged. In the case of a house, it is not practical to physically possess the property, but the creditor assumes part ownership, registered as a lien, which prevents the owner from completing the sale of a property until the debt is discharged. Even if the selling price is reduced by the amount of the outstanding lien, the property becomes difficult to sell.

The purpose of a lien is to protect contractors, subcontractors, and suppliers who invest materials and labor in a property, and to ensure that they are paid. For example, say you are building an addition and hire a contractor. Let's say he doesn't pay the subcontractor he hired to excavate and pour the concrete footings. The subcontractor can register a lien, equivalent to the sum he is owed for his work and materials, against your property within forty-five days from the date the work was completed, and the only way to discharge it is for you to pay the amount directly to the creditor or, if the matter has progressed, deposit the amount in court. You then have to recover the disputed amount from the contractor, which could be a very protracted exercise.

In order to prevent this from happening to you, you should hold back ten percent of what you owe to your contractor for the same forty-five days the supplier or contractor has to register the lien, and you should hold back that percentage from each payment, not just the last. Don't feel guilty over the holdbacks — they are legal and contractors expect them.

Before starting any work, you should have a contract with a payment schedule that clearly outlines due dates and amounts, including holdback arrangements. Ideally, it should be checked by a lawyer or other knowledgeable adviser. Before you make final payment, check that the job is satisfactorily completed and that no liens have been attached to the property.

A lien search is conducted at your Land Registry Office forty-five days after the work has been completed, and you needn't have any legal experience. The fee is generally around five dollars, and the staff will show you where to look and how to operate a microfiche file. A lawyer will be happy to do it for you, but will inevitably require a contribution to his expenses in addition to the search fee. If no lien has been registered, you can make final payment of the holdback.

If a lien has been registered, and you don't know why, then you must withhold any further payment and investigate immediately.

Let's assume you have had an extension added to the back of your house, and that the work progressed seemingly without a hitch. Payments were always made on time, and no complaints were ever made to you or witnessed by you between any of the workers or subtrades. You are satisfied that the job is completely finished, and all minor deficiencies brought to the attention of the general contractor have been adequately rectified. The forty-five-day holdback period has now passed, and you are keen to settle the balance of the bill. So, you pay a visit to the Land Registry Office.

To your amazement, the search reveals that a lien for $1,328.00 has been registered against your property by the framers. Fortunately, the amount you held back exceeds the amount of the lien, but the matter still needs to be addressed with little delay.

You should communicate first with your general contractor, since he is responsible to you for any shortcomings by his employees and subcontractors.

Your agreement is also signed by him, and he will want to resolve any problem that will delay his final payment. Copies will be sent to the subcontractor so there is no danger of his not knowing what is going on. Your first letter should be something like this:

---

321 Isore Street
Skrudup
T6M 9C2

Delade & Riptof Construction Ltd.
12 Tialmissin Road
Skrudup
T2Z 8B1

November 8, 1991

For the attention of Adam Nusants, President

Dear Adam,

I have just returned from the Land Registry Office, where I was shocked to learn that a lien, #X375567, was registered against my property on September 17, 1991, by Rottwud Framing Inc., the subcontractor you hired to frame my addition in early September. The amount of the claim is $1,328.00.

This is a very serious charge, and I require your immediate explanation of the circumstances that precipitated this wholly unjustified action.

Unless you take whatever steps are necessary to have your subcontractor discharge the lien within seven days and you furnish me with documentation in confirmation, I shall be obliged to deal with them directly.

Until this matter is resolved to my satisfaction, there is no question of my settling the outstanding balance of $2,673.00 due your company on November 11. In fact, should I have to negotiate with and/or pay Rottwud Framing, any necessary payments, plus my expenses, will be deducted from the said balance.

Perhaps you would be good enough to deal with this at once.

Yours sincerely,

Lena Nevva

c.c. Terry Fied, President, Rottwud Framing Inc.

Mr. Nusants will want to deal with the framers himself — he may be able to settle for less than the amount of the lien. Certainly, he will want to do so as quickly as possible so that he will get his last payment from you.

However, Mr. Nusants calls you with an explanation. He claims there was a dispute between him and his sub concerning the amount of work needed for the framing, which affected the price for the job they had agreed on verbally. Mr. Fied had insisted on being paid more, and had billed for the extra amount. Mr. Nusants had disputed the new figure, and had only paid the original price, leaving $1,328.00 outstanding, which was duly registered as a lien by the disgruntled Mr. Fied.

Disagreements between a contractor and his subcontractors are not your responsibility, and any disputes between them should be solved at their expense, not yours. You have a fixed-price contract, and unless you agreed to any extras subsequent to the date it was signed, that is all you are required to pay. Should any unforeseen problem affect that price, then the general contractor should negotiate an adjustment with you prior to completing the work. But an error in estimating labor or materials for a straightforward framing project does not fall into this category, and you must insist that unless Mr. Nusants settles his quarrel within the seven days specified in your letter, you will have to take your case to Mr. Fied without further notice.

If the contractor is still unsuccessful in negotiating with his sub, and the lien is not discharged in good time, then you will have to write to the lien holder, as follows:

---

321 Isore Street
Skrudup
T6M 9C2

Rottwud Framing Inc
90 Turmight Avenue
Skrudup
T4V 5T8

November 16, 1991

For the attention of Terry Fied, President

Dear Mr. Fied,

As you are aware, I have written to, and subsequently spoken to Adam Nusants of Delade & Riptof Construction Ltd., concerning the discharge of Lien #X375567 registered by your company against my property. I am informed that your account with Delade & Riptof is the subject of a dispute, which occasioned your charge in the amount of $1,328.00.

I am naturally far from happy to have to deal with your claim, particularly since the subject of your disagreement

is something over which I have no control and do not
intend to become involved in.

I am, however, obliged to take action to ensure that the lien
on my property is discharged, and since Mr. Nusants seems
unable to do this on my behalf, I am applying to you directly.

As soon as I receive your written and signed confirmation
that on receipt of my remittance of an irrevocable
payment of $1,328.00, you will undertake complete and
final discharge of lien #X375567 against my property, I
will make the required payment without delay.

Kindly confirm your intentions at your earliest
convenience, and I will respond accordingly.

Yours sincerely,

Lena Nevva

c.c. Adam Nusants, President, Delade & Riptof
Construction Ltd.

The copy to Mr. Nusants will suffice to let him know that, unless he is able to
resolve his dispute with Mr. Fied, his final payment will suffer to the tune of
$1,328.00, plus your expenses.

A sound move would be to meet Mr. Fied at the Land Registry Office, where
you could pay him and supervise the relevant documentation simultaneously.
If this is not convenient, make sure your check is exchanged for a receipted
document, which clearly describes the transaction to which it applies.

7

An Apple a Day: Taking on the Professions

Most of us have developed an unhealthy dose of awe for the professionals and a high tolerance for unprofessional behaviour and business practices. A well-worded letter will be highly effective when dealing with doctors, lawyers, dentists, teachers, and others, unaccustomed as they are to receiving correspondence from mere mortals.

EXCESSIVE WAITING TIME FOR AN APPOINTMENT

The medical profession generally enjoys an excellent reputation for looking after the best interests of its customers, or patients. This is to be expected; by definition medicine is a caring vocation.

It takes time for a doctor and patient to get to know and understand each other, and you should allow your doctor's office ample opportunity to show its mettle. Should you feel there is a serious problem, don't be afraid to transfer to another practice. If you are having problems, try to discuss them with the physician, before switching your allegiance. Any reasonable practitioner should be open to suggestions, and might welcome an opportunity to hear patients' views. Start by telling him or her the good points before you broach the negatives. If it is impossible or inconvenient to change doctors, then you are in an especially difficult situation, and you will have to remedy your differences with considerable tact.

Let's say that you have moved to a small community where the choice of physicians is limited, and you have a medical condition that requires you to make frequent visits to the doctor, often on an emergency basis. However, there is only one doctor in this community, and she can barely keep up with the demand for her services, with the result that there is a backlog of patients. You frequently find that you are unable to get an appointment when you need one.

You have discussed the problem with your physician, and she has agreed that you need attention as soon as possible and assured you her receptionist would give you priority in future. However, you continue to experience extensive delays. Again you mention the problem to the doctor, who tells you that there is such a backlog of patients, some of whom also require urgent attention, that her receptionist cannot guarantee much improvement. Furthermore, she tells you, good receptionists are difficult to find, let alone keep, and she does not want to upset the receptionist by pressuring her when she is already frantically busy. She barely has time to see her patients as it is, and if she had to hire and train a new receptionist, life would become impossible.

You sympathize with the doctor's predicament. But since you cannot do anything about your condition, you have no alternative but to find a way to receive priority help without causing friction between you and the doctor, and without alienating the receptionist. As soon as you return home from your visit, you write to the doctor.

---

555 Koffing Lane
Apartment 607
Sematree
R1P 9I1

Dr. Paula Bludd
Hurnia Building
Bakurts Street
Sematree
R1C 3D5

November 13, 1991

Dear Dr. Bludd,

As ever, I much appreciated your attention to my continuing stomach condition during my visit to your office this afternoon, and I eagerly await the day when your expert treatment results in my restoration to full health. Until such time, however, I am very concerned that my recovery is not being helped by the three- to four-day delays in getting an appointment with you.

I know you are working under great pressure, and I understand the difficulty your receptionist has in finding me a space in your busy schedule, often at short notice.

Nonetheless, it is necessary for me to be seen without delay because postponing treatment worsens my condition, which in turn prolongs my recovery and makes necessary even more visits to you. I can't afford the additional time off work this would entail, nor can I endure the added discomfort. And you don't need the extra workload.

With this in mind, the next time I have to call for an appointment and one is not available for several days, I will suggest a hopefully suitable time for the same day, or at most the very next day, to your receptionist. If an acceptable time does not appear possible, I will arrive in any case, in the hope of a cancellation or your very kindly being able to find a few extra minutes to fit me in.

With best regards,

Yours sincerely,

Mel Ingerrer

P.S. Surely the health authority is responsible for ensuring that the number of patients in your care is not so large that you can only see them when you have time, rather than when you need to? I should be happy to lobby them on your behalf, if you think it would help.

The postscript is optional, depending on whether you think your doctor will respond positively without "head office" being dragged into the debate. This is not phrased as a threat, of course, but as a sympathetic and concerned offer to bring in some outside assistance. The letter itself is straightforward, and expresses your appreciation of the medical facility and understanding of its problems. At the same time, you assert that you will not tolerate any more delays in your treatment, and that you intend to turn up and will refuse to leave until you have been seen. And this is what you must do.

The next time you need an appointment, if you are not given an appointment for that day, inform the receptionist that you will be arriving at a specific time. Try to choose a convenient time, although you will almost certainly inconvenience the doctor to some extent no matter what time you appear.

When you arrive, politely but firmly confirm your intentions, and take a seat until you are attended to. No doctor is going to lock up the office at the end of the day with a patient still sitting in the waiting room. Neither is she going to ask the police to remove a sick patient waiting for treatment because she is late for dinner!

Once you have established yourself as a determined customer, future appointments should be easily arranged. Once you are being seen at the short notice you demand, it would do no harm to express your appreciation to the doctor. Just a short note will suffice.

---

555 Koffing Lane
Apartment 607
Sematree
R1P 9I1

Dr. Paula Bludd
Hurnia Building
Bakurts Street
Sematree
R1C 3D5

December 5, 1991

Dear Dr. Bludd,

I just wanted you to know how much I appreciated being seen by you at short notice yesterday.

It is a great relief to know that you share my concern over the question of deferred appointments, and I trust that future visits to your office will continue to be afforded the same kind consideration.

Again, many thanks.

Yours sincerely,

Mel Ingerrer

If you are engaged in a dispute with someone with whom you are obliged to continue a relationship after the disputed matter has been resolved, sending a note of appreciation, if conditions so merit, will often help put the relationship back on track and prevent a recurrence of the problem. And prevention, as your physician will readily concur, is invariably better than cure.

DENTIST CHARGES FOR "HYGIENE EDUCATION"

The anxiety you experience in a dentist's chair is often nothing compared to your reaction when the bill is presented. Unless you have dental insurance, preferably with the premiums financed by someone other than you, payment can create a painful cavity in your wallet. Dentists' rates do vary, and it pays to shop around.

Before any dental work is agreed to, you should find out exactly what the charges will be. Assuming that the price will be the same as the last visit could be a costly mistake, one that can be easily avoided by making a quick telephone call to discover the current charge. If the amount quoted seems high, or has increased substantially since your last visit for similar treatment, call a couple of other practitioners to see if the price is competitive. If you discover that the same job can be done elsewhere for less, but you would prefer to remain with a dentist you know and trust, call him back and ask him to explain the difference. Surprisingly, rates charged by the "professions" can be negotiated, and while it is not realistic to bargain for a discount on every occasion, it is certainly worth questioning a charge that is above the going rate, or has risen by an excessive amount.

The best way to save money on dental work, of course, is to practice preventive maintenance. This, as everyone knows, includes brushing after meals and avoiding sweets. Many dentists routinely educate their patients, especially their juvenile ones, in the best method of cleaning teeth with a correctly angled brush. This usually takes thirty seconds and is carried out by the dentist or hygienist during treatment. And it seems that this demonstration is now commonly billed for under the heading Dental Education. The nominal charge for this invaluable thirty-second demonstration of the latest scientific breakthrough in tooth-brushing technology is usually no more than eight or ten dollars, or a modest $960 to $1,200 an hour!

Patients' initial reaction to this minor item is annoyance, but since the amount is relatively insignificant when compared to the cost of the rest of the treatment, they usually stop short of calling the dental office to voice their objection. After all, what's eight dollars nowadays?

Well, if you have a family of five, and you visit the dentist every six months, it's $80 to $100 per year — just to be reminded that it's the end with the stiff plastic hairs that you put the toothpaste on, not the bald section, and that you grip it with that handy appendage at the end of your arm.

As for the dentist, if he sees an average of sixteen patients a day, five days a week, the education is worth $33,280 to $41,600 a year. These charges may not be covered under a dental plan, for insurance is normally limited to actual dental treatment only. Yet, the dentist could easily afford to reverse the charge for the few patients who protest. The question is, how to go about it?

The most effective way is to write a short note of dissent, and then send it, along with the invoice *unpaid*. Your returning the invoice requires the dentist to respond, for the bill has now effectively not been sent, and if it hasn't been sent, it can't be paid. Your impact on his cash flow will be maximized. Your missive could look something like this:

---

87 Aggerney Avenue
Bytankel
H5G 2S7

Dr. Hal Otosiz
Dental Surgeon
200 Drilphang Street
Bytankel
H7J 1Y9

November 13, 1991

Dear Dr. Otosiz,

I am returning your bill dated November 8, 1991, for dental treatment. My reason for doing so is to give you the opportunity to credit the three charges, at ten dollars each, for Dental Education. Neither of my two children or I have ever requested such "education." Nor was it ever offered as an option or were we ever warned we would be charged for this.

We do vaguely recall your hygienist briefly waving a toothbrush about during our respective visits, but I can scarcely imagine that this could be the items to which your bill refers. Even if I am mistaken, then payment is still clearly out of the question, for the reasons described above.

Please confirm in writing that future visits will not be followed by repeated charges of this type. Your account will be settled as soon as I am in receipt of a corrected invoice.

Yours sincerely,

Phil McAvitty

That should produce the desired result. Since the amount involved is relatively small, neither side will want to engage in protracted correspondence, and the credit should be speedily dispatched. In the remote likelihood that the dentist tries to convince you of the validity of the billing, and you feel sufficiently incensed to stick to your guns, then a further letter should be sent, as follows:

---

87 Aggerney Avenue
Bytankel
H5G 2S7

Dr. Hal Otosiz
Dental Surgeon
200 Drilphang Street
Bytankel
H7J 1Y9

November 28, 1991

Dear Dr. Otosiz,

I have received your letter dated November 26, together with your invoice #5645. Your explanation that Dental Education is a standard procedure practiced by most dentists is totally unsatisfactory. Whether your assertion is accurate is of no interest to me, and is entirely beside the point, for three reasons:

(1) The "Education" was not requested.

(2) The "Education" was not notified by you, and was commenced spontaneously.

(3) No notice of any cost was ever mentioned or made known to me, until shown on your invoice.

Enclosed is my check for $473.98, in full settlement of your invoice, less the Dental Education charges, which have been deducted. Please let me have your receipt confirming that the account is now paid in full.

Alternatively, if you would prefer that I seek an independent opinion concerning these charges, I am more than willing to bring the matter to the attention of Den Turze, president of the Federal Dental Association.

Yours sincerely,

Phil McAvitty

Encl.

Note that you have not actually sent anything to the Dental Association yet; you are merely asking whether Dr. Otosiz would like you to do so! Also, you have paid all the money to which he is entitled, which leaves the balance hardly worth the bother of further debate. Why waste more time writing back and forth when the money can still be collected in multiple units from other patients who won't put up as much of a fight as you have? The dentist will likely not "educate" you in future, but if he does, and charges you again, just repeat the process until he finally gets the message.

LAWYER OVERCHARGES FOR SERVICES

It is hoped that your skills in communication will help to resolve most of the injustices life sends your way. Inevitably, though, nearly everyone will need to consult a lawyer about some matter at some time. Not necessarily for the advice or collection of a claim for damages, of course, but to perform other less unpleasant duties that require professional experience and expertise.

You should seek a lawyer who is capable, expeditious, and trustworthy, and whose fees are reasonable. (Some suggestions for selecting counsel are outlined in chapter 10.) There is still no guarantee, however, that at the end of the day, the bill for legal fees will be entirely without surprises. Frequently the bewildering terminology employed by the legal profession extends to the bill for services, which can make interpretation and confirmation of any previously advised fees very difficult.

If discrepancies are minor, and you have otherwise had a smooth journey through the process that precipitated the bill, then a telephone call to the lawyer's office will probably be all that is required to clarify the account. But what if the bill defies analysis, what if the amount billed is much more than expected, and you suspect it is not due to an accounting error?

Few clients are eager to cross swords with their lawyers, particularly if the lawyers have just demonstrated their skill at subduing the opposition. How you question the account requires careful thought and planning. In this case, you do not care to pay the excess charges, so you send the invoice back.

The logic behind returning an incorrect invoice is quite simple, but nonetheless important. Sending it back shows tangible evidence of rejection, and puts the onus on the sender to react, as you cannot be expected to pay an account that is no longer in your possession. It is also useful to highlight in color or underline the items you are querying. A conscientious secretary may not want to send the same bill back if it looks too scruffy. Since it will have to be retyped anyway, perhaps it will be easier to make the corrections at the same time. A small point possibly, but it pays to think of as many angles as possible.

The returned invoice will have to be qualified by an accompanying letter, which might look something like this:

---

                                        345 Skydde Row
                                        Lorscam
                                        F3X 2V4

Byte, Deth, Kurcing & Mallishus, Solicitors
Gillatine Tower
Virelants Street
Lorscam
X7D 1K2

                                        November 12, 1991

For the attention of Angela Deth

Dear Angela,

I have received your bill dated November 11 for
$1,687.00, covering your acting on my behalf in the
matter of drafting the lease for and securing the assets of
my recently acquired private zoo.

As far as I was aware, the transaction was no more
complicated or prolonged than we anticipated, and I am
therefore unable to understand why I have been charged

so much more than the $900.00 you originally estimated. I appreciate that an estimate may be subject to some adjustment either way, but to have almost doubled without notice or explanation is quite unacceptable.

I am returning your invoice herewith. You will note that I have marked the items that I cannot reconcile or that have been charged over the agreed price.

Kindly forward an amended account in line with your quotation of $900.00, and if there are any extraordinary items you feel justified in submitting, please show them separately, and describe them in complete detail in a covering letter.

As soon as I consider the account satisfactory, I will pay it by return post.

Yours sincerely,

Wal Ruses

Encl.

If you confirm any estimates in writing prior to engaging the lawyer, any such large increase in the lawyer's fee will be difficult to justify. A detailed breakdown may be a burden to the lawyer, but the greater the detail, the better able you will be to dispute the amounts. Finally, you have promised immediate payment once you agree to the account.

Usually lawyers' fees, although theoretically calculated on a fixed hourly rate, can be negotiated successfully, with the firm still making a handsome profit. For example, a lot of the mundane work in the purchase of your zoo will probably have been performed by a junior, who would command a low salary. The hourly rate charged to you, however, would not necessarily reflect this. A lot of "rounding-up" might have also occurred; an eight-minute telephone call invoiced at a quarter of an hour, for instance. So there is plenty of flexibility, particularly if you are quite prepared to stand your ground. You might be prepared to show some flexibility yourself; you should probably accept a variance of between ten and fifteen percent without making too much of a fuss.

Should you not be offered the reduction to which you feel entitled, there are other incentives that can be mentioned in your next letter. Lawyers generally dislike arguing over bills, particularly when the option to involve a third party is offered to them. The two least-popular third parties are the law society, which will quickly respond to a complaint made to them, and the court, where you can have the bill assessed (taxed) by a court official. The fact that you are aware of the existence of both these facilities is well worth mentioning.

But before you send the next letter, you must decide whether to continue to withhold all the amount claimed, or just pay the portion you consider appropriate. If you pay nothing, you will doubtless encourage a quick response, since your lawyers will be keener to collect a larger amount than a smaller one. Also, you will have the benefit of any interest accruing in your account, or the money might be temporarily useful for some other purpose. On the other hand, your lawyers may suspect that you are procrastinating because you cannot afford to pay, or simply do not wish to. You will not want to have them doubt your motives and change their response from defensive to offensive.

If, instead, you remit the amount you are prepared to pay, making it clear that this is absolutely all that they are going to get, you will find your position considerably improved. You will have shown that you do have the money, and are willing to pay, provided a reasonable compromise is possible. If they know the amount sent is adequate compensation for the work performed, they will probably not wish to engage in further time-consuming correspondence for the balance, particularly if you offer to have the disputed amount decided by arbitration. Your next letter should therefore be something like this:

---

345 Skydde Row
Lorscam
F3X 2V4

Byte, Deth, Kurcing & Mallishus, Solicitors
Gillatine Tower
Virelants Street
Lorscam
X7D 1K2

November 28, 1991

For the attention of Angela Deth

Dear Angela,

I have received your letter dated November 26, and returned bill dated November 11. I regret that I cannot reconcile or agree with your justification for the extraordinary difference between your estimate made on September 23, and the actual amount invoiced.

I therefore enclose a check for $900.00 in full and final payment for the services provided, per the estimate upon which I based my contract with you, in good faith. Kindly forward a receipt at your earliest convenience, confirming that my obligations to your practice have been met in full.

If you do not feel obliged to respect our original agreement, please let me know by return post, and I will bring the matter to the attention of Madge E. Straight, President of the Law Society. If she so advises, I will bring your invoice before the court, to permit this dispute to be settled by taxation.

I look forward to your early advice.

Yours sincerely,

Wal Ruses

Encl.

You have made it very difficult for the lawyers not to agree to your terms since they now have a substantial part of the bill paid, with the threat of unwelcome intervention if they persist in claiming the balance. The chances of further opposition are therefore very remote, but if you do experience any more unreasonable demands, then send your file to the Law Society, with a covering letter, as follows:

345 Skydde Row
Lorscam
F3X 2V4

Law Society
555 Thumskrue Avenue
Bribarry
R4B 7M5

December 4, 1991

For the attention of Madge E. Straight, President

Dear Ms. Straight,

I am enclosing copies of recent correspondence between
Byte, Deth, Kurcing & Mallishus, Solicitors, and me. As you
can see, I have been billed for almost twice the amount
originally quoted by Ms. Deth, with no apparent justification.

Attempts to reconcile this dispute have not met with
success, and I would be most grateful if you could favor
me with your valuable opinion as to whether I should
seek arbitration through taxation in court, or whether
you are personally authorized to intervene in such cases.

I look forward to your early response, and thank you in
anticipation.

Yours sincerely,

Wal Ruses

Encls.

c.c. Byte, Deth, Kurcing, & Mallishus, Solicitors

The law society may write to the lawyers suggesting that it would be in
everyone's interest for them to settle the dispute as soon as possible, or

they may offer one of any number of alternative solutions for your consideration. Their advice or comments are generally sound, and should be carefully considered. Naturally, you are not bound to agree with their opinion, and if you are not satisfied with their intervention, you have little to lose by taking the account to the court office for taxation.

If the court official decides that you have been charged an excessive amount, then he may amend the bill to a more realistic figure. Incidentally, he cannot increase the account, should he decide that you appear to have been undercharged!

TEACHER GIVES UNFAIR MARK

Teaching is a demanding vocation, requiring a considerable amount of knowledge, and the skill and patience to pass on information to children of different ages, varying social and ethnic backgrounds, and infinite mixture of aptitudes, attitudes, and interests. The teachers have to do their best to ensure that each pupil leaves school at the end of the day with more or less the same amount of knowledge — no small task when young minds are blessed with different degrees of resistance and talent.

Teachers must constantly assess their young charges in order to establish and maintain a consistent level of learning. A good teacher will regard each pupil as an individual, which inevitably means that to some extent each child will be treated differently, even though such differences may be subtle. Individual attention should, of course, be restricted to helping a child to overcome any difficulties he or she may have in keeping up with the rest of the class, and should not extend to having any evident bias for or against a pupil.

Let us say your youngster has received consistently low marks for assignments for no apparent reason — assignments were always neat, handed in on time, grammatical, and well researched. Other pupils had received higher marks for similar work. You have discussed the problem at home, and you have asked your child to bring home some of the others' papers for comparison, which he does. You examine them carefully, and feel your boy's paper looks better than the ones with higher marks.

You are at a loss to explain the variance, but you suspect that the teacher does not care for your son; he is inclined to be rather lively, and has a reputation for being a practical joker. You recognize that his disruptive behavior merits some form of correction, but his academic performance should not be affected. However, at this stage you are only speculating, and should not assume anything until your suspicions are bolstered by more tangible evidence.

You and your son decide that he will approach the teacher himself, and he does so the next day. During an opportune moment, he confronts the teacher, spreading out before her the comparison papers and his own. He asks her to explain what caused his paper to earn lower marks than his classmates', because he is anxious to improve his marks. The teacher, unimpressed by this affront to her authority, responds that all papers were marked fairly, and that she is not obliged to discuss the marks in detail with her pupils.

That evening, your crestfallen son describes his experience to you. You decide to wait for the next set of marks before proceeding further since you have only seen one paper that deserved a better mark, even though your son claims there were others. And indeed, the next paper again seems to have been marked unfairly. This confirms that something is amiss, and you decide that a letter, written by your son, is in order. You do not yet approach the principal because you want to give the teacher an opportunity to qualify her actions and to correct them without further intervention. Your son could write something like this:

---

23 Skoller Avenue
Yuniver City
T9H 0N0

Weirig Norrant Middle School
55 Dispare Street
Yuniver City
T6G 2W2

November 15, 1991

For the attention of Miss Jean Eyuss

Dear Miss Eyuss,

As you are aware, I am a Grade 6 student at the above School, where I am privileged to have you as one of my teachers.

I have become increasingly concerned over the past few

months, however, that the marks you have been giving me are considerably lower than my work merited. In fact, I have compared my papers with those of several of my classmates, and it appears that they are receiving higher marks for papers that are equal or inferior to mine.

I have discussed this at length with my parents, who naturally share my concerns, and are keen to discover the reason for this. I tried to make you aware of my anxiety last week, but you did not consider the matter worthy of debate at the time. Perhaps this letter will convince you that I take my education seriously and in return I expect similar consideration from my teachers.

Your early reply to my concern over low marks will therefore be appreciated.

Yours sincerely,

Toby Ornotobe

There might be advantages in the parents' writing the letter themselves; a teacher will likely react more favorably to an articulate parent than to one of the dozens of whining kids to whose incessant complaints she has of necessity acquired a deaf ear over the years! But the letter clearly states that you are aware of your child's concerns and the terminology in it obviously suggests parental assistance, so the impact should not be diluted. Besides, it is good to teach a child how to correctly handle the innumerable problems he will have to face in adult life as early as he is able to understand the principles.

The teacher will have to react to this letter, if only because the experience of receiving it has likely been something of a shock! She may correctly infer that ignoring articulation like this promises unwelcome confrontation, and a chastened discussion with Toby, followed by improved marks, can be anticipated in quick order.

Should the marks not improve, and you can still see no reason why they are so low, then it is time to involve the school principal. She could be addressed as follows:

23 Skoller Avenue
Yuniver City
T9H 0N0

Weirig Norrant Middle School
55 Dispare Street
Yuniver City
T6G 2W2

December 4, 1991

For the attention of Ms. A.B. Cees, Principal

Dear Ms. Cees,

I recently had occasion to write (copy enclosed) to Miss
Jean Eyuss, my Grade 6 teacher, concerning low marks I
have been receiving for my assignments. I regret to say
that my letter has not generated the requested improvement
in her assessment of my work, and my parents and I are
agreed that your personal intervention may now be
appropriate.

I find that concentration on my studies is adversely
affected by the prospect of results receiving scant
recognition, and would therefore appreciate your opinion
on the matter at your earliest convenience.

Thank you in anticipation.

Yours sincerely,

Toby Ornotobe

Encl.

c.c. Miss Jean Eyuss

This should prompt an independent investigation, and you have every reason
to expect a solution to be reached without delay.

After the matter has been resolved, your son should be discouraged from enthusiastically describing his "victory" to all and sundry, to avoid unnecessary embarrassment to the parties concerned and further friction between the teacher and him. Instead, in order to improve the now somewhat strained relations that probably exist between Miss Eyuss and him, he would do well to pour oil on troubled waters by sending her a note of appreciation, if the matter has been permanently resolved.

---

23 Skoller Avenue
Yuniver City
T9H ONO

Weirig Norrant Middle School
55 Dispare Street
Yuniver City
T6G 2W2

December 18, 1991

For the attention of Ms. A.B. Cees, Principal

Dear Ms. Cees,

Further to your and Miss Eyuss's meeting with my parents and me earlier this month, I am writing to express my appreciation of your interest in my studies.

I shall continue to do my best to demonstrate that your valuable assistance will contribute much to my work. Thank you both again for addressing my concerns so promptly.

Yours sincerely,

Toby Ornotobe

c.c. Miss Jean Eyuss

8

Unaccommodating Accommodation: Tenants vs Landlords

Anyone who rents property must deal from time to time with the landlord. Many landlords are quick to respond to their tenants' needs; others need written reminders of their obligations every time a problem arises.

LANDLORD RAISES RENT BEYOND GUIDELINES

Most provinces and states have legislation that limits either rent increases or the frequency with which those increases can be applied, or both. Usually an increase can only be set once a year, in the same month, but this may not apply if, for instance, a tenant moves six months after the rent was raised, when a landlord might be allowed to establish a higher rent with the new tenant.

If legislation covering increases is in effect, then the rate of inflation usually dictates the percentage increase allowed. Such an increase is usually valid for one year, until reassessed according to the new inflation statistics. Additional factors may affect the set rate, but generally increases much over the rate of inflation are not allowed.

Both landlords and tenants should be familiar with the prevailing legislation in their area; most authorities publish information outlining both parties' responsibilities, or at least have a department that can answer any questions on the subject. You should be able to find the number of your local legislating body in the government pages of your telephone directory, or your local library should be of assistance.

Rent controls seem geared to favor tenants, and occasionally some frustrated landlords are tempted to find ways to raise rents beyond the legal limits. Sometimes these landlords have indeed incurred genuine extraordinary expenses, such as essential, major building repairs or renovations, which justify the need for increased income. But some landlords carry out minimal renovations in order to qualify for larger than normal rent increases. They may even upgrade the building against the tenants' wishes, and then apply for an excessive increase, which the housing authorities may well see as justified if the expenditure can be shown to have been necessary or desirable.

Replacing hallway carpets that are full of holes, and repairing and painting the walls, for instance, should not justify a rent increase above the legislated guidelines, since this would be considered routine upkeep. On the other hand, upgrading windows, kitchen and bathroom cabinetry, tiles and flooring may indeed qualify for increased rents.

Once any upgrading has been completed, tenants may be unable to stop permission being granted for large rent increases. The best way to prevent such increases is to react *before* the work is started. Tenants should form an association, open a bank account, and collect donations from each resident to fight the intended work order. Combatting this type of action will require specialized knowledge, and the money accumulated could be used to appoint legal counsel familiar with this type of problem. The amount each tenant should contribute need not be substantial, especially if the building is a large one. If your campaign is successful, the expenditure will be insignificant compared to what your future rents might have been. Selecting competent counsel is essential, of course, and some suggestions on how to do this are outlined in chapter 10.

Say you live in a building in a part of the country where increases are limited to six percent per annum. Your landlord sends you his regular notice of the annual increase, expressed as a monetary amount, and you and your trusty abacus soon discover the increase to be fifteen percent — well over the legal limits. There is no explanation with the notification.

You call your local housing or rental authority to confirm that the ceiling is still six percent, and to verify that it has not been raised recently. Having received assurance that the set limit is indeed still six percent, your next move is to ask the landlord to explain why he has exceeded the legal amount permitted. This may be done by phone, but it is far better to deal with the matter in writing. To encourage a quick reply, return the notice with your letter; the landlord will know that you cannot be expected to comply with the content if it is no longer in your possession. Remember to make a good, legible photocopy first — you may need it later. Reply to his note of increase as follows:

788 Gowjusall Street
Apartment 411
Nomor Bux
R6Y 2S5

Skweazemdry Properties Ltd.
90 Menislumms Avenue
Nomor Bux
R2Y 5H6

November 26, 1991

For the attention of Cary Abigwolit, President

Dear Mr. Abigwolit,

Enclosed please find your notification dated November 19,
informing me of a rent increase for my apartment.

I see that you propose to increase my current rent of
$624.00 by $93.60, to a new total of $717.60,
commencing January 1, 1992. There would appear to be
an error in the calculation of this figure, for the increase
you are seeking is fifteen percent. As you must be aware,
current legislation allows a maximum increase of six
percent, which permits you to increase my rent by only
$37.44, to a total of $661.44.

Perhaps you would be good enough to send me a new
notification that complies with these binding guidelines,
which will enable me to respond to your requested
increase with more favorable consideration.

Yours sincerely,

Terry Blepour

At this point, while there is a possibility of a mathematical error, you do
not yet send a copy to the authorities responsible for setting the guidelines. Rent at the new rate is not due for six weeks, so there is plenty of

time to send copies of your correspondence to the authorities later if necessary. In case the landlord is just taking a chance you are unfamiliar with prevailing guidelines, your letter should assure him that he has underestimated you.

But you soon receive a letter from the landlord in which he quotes (or misquotes) a section of the legislation under which increases above six percent are permitted. It is then time to take advantage of your local authorities. Again, check the landlord's claim first in case it has indeed been approved by the authorities. A telephone call quickly confirms that the increase has not been approved, and you now reply to the landlord, and send a copy together with all previous documentation to the authority.

---

788 Gowjusall Street
Apartment 411
Nomor Bux
R6Y 2S5

Skweazemdry Properties Ltd.
90 Menislumms Avenue
Nomor Bux
R2Y 5H6

December 1, 1991

For the attention of Cary Abigwolit, President

Dear Mr. Abigwolit,

I am in receipt of your letter dated November 29, and have noted your reasons for seeking to raise my rent by fifteen percent instead of the legal limit of six percent. The Ministry of Housing confirms that your claim has no validity, and that you must reduce the increase to an amount not exceeding the legislated maximum.

Unless you are able to provide me with written evidence, in the form of documents from the ministry, clearly showing that you have been granted authorization to exceed the current limit, then I shall assume that my liability is six percent, and I will remit my monthly checks at that amount. Perhaps you would be good

enough to confirm my legal rent at your earliest
convenience.

Yours sincerely,

Terry Blepour

c.c. Marge Inalhike, Director, Ministry of Housing

If you do not have a tenants' association, you might want to help your fellow residents dispute the landlord's illegal claim when they are presented with the same increase. Their extra voices will help dissuade the landlord from making similar demands in the future. To this end you should photocopy your correspondence, and provide each resident with a set accompanied by the following covering letter:

---

788 Gowjusall Street
Apartment 411

December 1, 1991

Dear Fellow Resident,

As the enclosed will demonstrate, the landlord is trying to
raise the rent for my apartment above the current legal
limit, and if he has not already done so, may well be pro-
posing to do the same for all tenants in this building.

The Ministry of Housing has confirmed that we do not have
to pay any amount over six percent, and I thought you
might like to see my correspondence so far to help you for-
mulate your own protest if an illegal demand is received.

Yours faithfully,

Terry Blepour

Encl.

If the landlord does not send you an amended notice of increase at the legal rate, or persists with his original demands, then you should seek intervention from the ministry, as follows:

788 Gowjusall Street
Apartment 411
Nomor Bux
R6Y 2S5

Ministry of Housing
Ovastafd Building
111 Neppatizm Street
Ollar Bux
R4Y 1Q3

December 15, 1991

For the attention of Marge Inalhike, Director

Dear Ms. Inalhike,

As you will see from the enclosed correspondence, my
landlord persists in demanding a rent increase for my
apartment, which I understand to be considerably in
excess of the limit imposed by your ministry. Perhaps
you would be good enough to write to him on my
behalf, since he seems unconvinced by my protests.

Until this matter is settled, do you advise that I continue
to pay my rent at (a) the present rate, (b) the present
rate plus six percent, or (c) the present rate plus the
demanded fifteen percent (in which case I would deduct
any amount that your binding decision deems illegal from
future payments)?

I look forward to hearing from you, and thank you in
anticipation.

Yours sincerely,

Terry Blepour

Encl.

c.c. Cary Abigwolit, Skweazemdry Properties Ltd.
     All residents of 788 Gowjusall Street

Your photocopying budget may not extend to furnishing your fellow tenants with continual updates of your efforts, but it will do no harm to make sure the ministry and the landlord know that they are contending with a considerable number of people.

The housing authority will now intervene on your behalf, and will probably advise that you pay the new rent with a six percent increase until a final verdict is reached. They may, of course, immediately advise all parties that no increase over six percent will be allowed under any circumstances. In either case, your efforts will have been worthwhile and effective, and your chastened landlord may think twice before acting in such a manner again.

RENTAL REBATE FOR DISTURBED ACCOMMODATION

The majority of apartment buildings are designed to comply with building codes and engineering specifications, not necessarily to win design awards. Standards vary according to market influences; buildings will have more facilities and be of better quality in expensive and sophisticated districts than those in areas that are less well off, which will inevitably be reflected in the landlord's rental charges.

Other conditions influence the standard of a particular unit or units, and these include the age of the building, the materials used to construct it, the size of the building, whether it has been converted from an older residential or commercial structure, and its proximity to outside influences that might affect the structure or comfort of the tenants. In an older apartment building, for example, traffic may have steadily increased over a number of years, or an adjoining property might have been rezoned for commercial use, raising the noise and pollution levels.

Generally, these are conditions over which the landlord has no control, and it is up to prospective tenants to take such matters into consideration before committing themselves to a rental agreement. Don't complain after moving into the premises about something beyond the landlord's control that was perfectly obvious at the time the unit was inspected. For instance, a basement apartment can hardly be expected to afford the same amount of natural light as a unit on the second floor. Such a shortcoming is inevitable, and readily evident before an agreement to rent is signed.

Anyone living in a high-density building should be prepared to be tolerant. No building is perfectly designed, is totally soundproofed against noise from outside or fellow residents, or has a magic system whereby necessary repairs are made before the need for them occurs.

Tenants invariably view paying rent with reluctance, and assume that the unfortunate landlord is a millionaire who has never had to do a stroke of work in his life and doesn't care about his tenants. This may be true in some cases, of course, but even if it isn't, the landlord is usually presumed guilty until (and sometimes, even when) proved innocent.

It can be difficult to ensure that all tenants in a building, particularly if it is a large one, will maintain standards at a high level, and you cannot reasonably expect a landlord to be totally successful in his selection of occupants. Inevitably, there are differences in the way various tenants conduct themselves, just as there are differences in the degree of responsibility exercised by landlords.

There are, however, occasions when a complaint is justified, and appropriate steps must be followed in order to obtain a satisfactory outcome without jeopardizing a tenancy agreement or one's relations with the landlord or fellow residents. A tenant should be entitled to "peaceful enjoyment of the premises," with all that such a stipulation implies, together with adequate maintenance, necessary repairs completed at acceptable times, temperature appropriate to the climate and local guidelines, and any other specified or legislated services that apply to a particular building.

Let's assume that you live in an apartment with hardwood floors, fixed to what you presume is a concrete subfloor. You can tolerate the inevitable noises — the odd door slammed in anger, unruly guests visiting a neighbor, someone dropping something. But a new tenant assumed residence in the apartment above you three weeks ago, and you haven't slept since. Despite the stipulation in the lease requiring tenants to install sufficient carpeting to prevent noise disturbing other tenants, you are still being disturbed at all hours by footsteps, furniture scraping, things being dropped, and other unidentifiable bangs and clatters.

Three weeks is enough time to allow for unpacking and arranging furniture, and installing of a carpet or adequate rugs; you are now entitled to request that your new neighbors afford consideration to their fellow residents. Before confronting your neighbors, however, you should keep a log of the times and severity of the disturbances. This will give your grievance credibility and may prove helpful later.

Your first contact with your neighbors must be carefully worded in order to persuade them that your grievance is very real, that resolving it is important to you, that you are sure that they are probably unaware that noise is so easily carried to adjoining suites, and that you are not the resident "radar" out to plague every tenant in the building with an endless repertoire of complaints. You could confront them in person, but this is not advisable since a resultant argument will not be to your advantage.

A better route would be to speak to the superintendent first, to register your complaint, and then to proceed on your own with a letter. Of course, you will keep the superintendent informed of your progress. Don't contact the landlord or his managing agent yet — give your neighbors the benefit of the doubt.

A short note introducing yourself and describing the circumstances that compelled you to write is your most appropriate course of action. Keep a copy of the letter, of course, but don't send copies to the superintendent or landlord at this stage, as you don't yet know whether their intervention is going to be required. Copies can be included with any subsequent correspondence, if necessary.

Your letter should read something like this:

Apartment 609
44 Vaguerant Street
Despair
T5H 3R3

The Occupant(s)
Apartment 709
44 Vaguerant Street
Despair
T5H 3R3

March 23, 1992

Dear Sir or Madam,

As will be evident from my address, my apartment is directly below the unit into which you moved at the beginning of March.

I regret that our first contact has to be in the form of a complaint, as I like to think that I am both tolerant and respectful of those with whom I share proximity, but I have to bring to your notice the persistent and disturbing noise that carries through from your apartment to my own, presumably as a result of your not having installed carpeting or rugs.

I appreciate that it takes time to unpack and arrange furniture and other household belongings, which is obviously difficult to accomplish in silence, but I do feel that after three weeks, the level of disturbance should be reduced to a minimum.

Please, therefore, install floor covering as necessary,
refrain from wearing hard-soled shoes on bare floors, and
ensure that movement of furniture and other effects does
not transmit excessive noise to my apartment.

Thank you in anticipation.

Yours faithfully,

Will Ushuddup

There is no need to mail the letter — just slip it under their door or through
a mail slot if there is one. If your neighbors are responsible citizens, then an
immediate reduction in the noise should be apparent. You might even receive
a note of explanation or a personal visit to pour oil over troubled waters.

If not, and the disturbance persists, or worse, the noise increases, then you
will have to gear up your efforts accordingly. Another, stronger letter is required, and a copy should be handed to the superintendent requesting that he
intervene on your behalf to ensure that the tenant complies without delay
with the conditions detailed in the letter. Be prepared to back up your complaint with notes from your log. Keep a copy for yourself, of course, but do
not send one to the landlord yet. Write as follows:

Apartment 609
44 Vaguerant Street
Despair
T5H 3R3

The Occupant(s)
Apartment 709
44 Vaguerant Street
Despair
T5H 3R3

March 27, 1992

Dear Sir or Madam,

My letter of March 23, requesting that you install carpeting in compliance with building regulations so that I
might be protected from the excessive and disturbing

noise emanating from your apartment, has not met with any evident reduction in the noise. On the contrary, the noise appears to have increased, and persists over even longer periods than previously.

Your immediate cooperation in reducing this unnecessary and distressing encroachment is again requested.

Your consideration in complying will be greatly appreciated.

Yours faithfully,

Will Ushuddup

c.c. Ben Dovabakwodz, Superintendent, 44 Vaguerant Street

Ask the superintendent to visit your apartment at a time when you know the occupant of the unit above will be at home, to confirm whether the noise is indeed excessive. Insist that you cannot tolerate the noise any longer, and that you will be contacting the landlord if it does not cease. Ascertain the name of the tenants, so that you can address them in any further communication.

If there is still no improvement, then a letter to the landlord is required:

Apartment 609
44 Vaguerant Street
Despair
T5H 3R3

Rak Anwruin Properties Ltd.
89 Prophit Avenue
Despair
T5K 6W2

March 29, 1992

For the attention of Justin Itferabuk, President

Dear Mr. Itferabuk,

Since March 1, when your new tenant, Mr. Des Truktiv, assumed occupancy of Apartment 709, directly above me, my right to "peaceful possession of the premises" has been seriously compromised by continuing loud and disturbing noises emanating from that apartment.

The main cause of the noise appears to be Mr. Truktiv's failure to install suitable carpeting on the hardwood floor as required in the regulations applying to this building and as specified in the Residential Tenancy act.

I did not register my complaint with Mr. Truktiv until March 23, when I wrote him a short request, since I know moving can be a chore and I assumed he might need some time to settle his belongings and to purchase a carpet. The noise persisted, however, and if anything became even more pronounced than ever.

I wrote again on March 27, and at that time gave a copy of my letter to the building superintendent, Mr. Dovabakwodz, requesting that he intervene on my behalf. Mr. Dovabakwodz also visited my apartment and confirmed that the noise from above was indeed excessive.

I have recorded consistent disturbance between the hours of 6:00 a.m and 8:30 a.m, and between 6:30 p.m and 1:30 a.m, Monday to Friday, and approximately 16 hours per day on weekends, between 10:00 a.m and 2:00 a.m the following morning. This is a total of seventy-nine hours per week, or nearly half of every day! To date there has been no reduction whatsoever in the level of noise.

This is absolutely unacceptable. Please promptly take whatever steps you consider appropriate to restore my entitlement to peaceful occupation. Thank you.

Yours sincerely,

Will Ushuddup

Encl.

c.c. Des Truktiv, tenant
     Ben Dovabakwodz, building superintendent

If the disturbance still persists after three or four days, and you have not been contacted by any of the recipients of your correspondence, ask the superintendent if he has received any instructions from the landlord, and if he has taken any further action on your behalf since you last spoke to him. If he has been asked by the landlord to intervene, and has done so, tell him that while you appreciate his efforts, they have not achieved any results as yet, and request that he speak to the offending tenants again.

If he hasn't heard from his employer, ask him to contact him for advice on how to handle the matter, and to again convey your continuing annoyance to the tenant as soon as possible. If there is still no improvement after a few days, write to the landlord again, as follows:

Apartment 609
44 Vaguerant Street
Despair
T5H 3R3

Rak Anwruin Properties Ltd.
89 Prophit Avenue
Despair
T5K 6W2

April 10, 1992

For the attention of Justin Itferabuk, President

Dear Mr. Itferabuk,

My letter of March 29, describing the intolerable noise I have endured in my apartment since March 1, 1992, has not produced any response or reduction in the continuing disturbance from the tenants directly above me. Neither have my requests for intervention to superintendent Ben Dovabakwodz proved to be of any benefit.

I am no longer able to endure this serious infringement of my right to peaceful possession of my apartment, and cannot understand why nothing has been done to rectify the matter.

Please be aware, therefore, that if the noise has not ceased by Friday, April 24, 1992, I will be obliged to search for alternative accommodation against my wishes. Until I do move out, I will be invoicing you at monthly intervals for a forty-five-percent refund on my rent, which represents the percentage of time my apartment is rendered unsuitable for the purpose for which it is intended, because of the actions of the tenant you have installed.

Please also be aware that should I be obliged to move through your failure to ensure that my premises are adequately protected from outside interference, I will be looking to you for all expenses incurred in moving to another address, including loss of wages if time off work is necessary; telephone, hydro, and cable television connection charges; change of address notifications; and any difference in rent if a comparable new apartment is more expensive than my current one.

I trust, therefore, that I may expect some positive action before April 24, failing which I shall have no option but to initiate the measures stated above.

Yours sincerely,

Will Ushuddup

c.c. Des Truktiv, tenant
    Ben Dovabakwodz, building superintendent

The prospect of having to finance your departure, together with receiving bills for rent refunds until you leave, should be sufficient to galvanize the landlord into action. (But don't risk eviction by actually reducing your rent payments.)

Instant silence should not be expected — it takes a few days to arrange carpeting. However, it would be reasonable for Mr. Truktiv to reduce the noise until the carpet does arrive. If by April 24, however, you have still not received a positive response from Mr. Itferabuk, then you must serve notice of your intention to move, and send your first invoice. In fairness to the landlord, you should invoice for your inconvenience only from the date you first notified him of the noise.

Write as follows:

Apartment 609
44 Vaguerant Street
Despair
T5H 3R3

Rak Anwruin Properties Ltd.
89 Prophit Avenue
Despair
T5K 6W2

April 24, 1992

For the attention of Justin Itferabuk, President

Dear Mr. Itferabuk,

Further to my letter of April 10, I am disappointed to
inform you that to date you have failed to address my
very real concerns, and that the excessive and intolerable
disturbance from the apartment directly above my own
unit continues unabated.

In consequence, therefore, and against my will, I am
obliged to seek alternative accommodation that offers me
the peaceful occupation to which I am legally entitled. As
soon as I have secured a suitable apartment, I will serve
formal notice of my intended date of vacation. Meanwhile,
I enclose my invoice for the suffering and inconvenience
experienced to date, and incurred through your having failed
to manage the building to standards required from a
responsible landlord. Early settlement will be appreciated.

Yours sincerely,

Will Ushuddup

Encl.

c.c. Des Truktiv, tenant
     Ben Dovabakwodz, building superintendent

It is important that you continue to send copies of your letters to all parties who are in a position to contribute a solution to the dispute. Notification of your increasing despair may yet produce the action needed to stay your intended departure. And should subsequent court proceedings be required, no one will be able to claim that they understood the matter to have been resolved.

It is not necessary to send duplicates of the invoice with the copy letters; notification that you are making a claim is quite sufficient. The invoice may look something like this:

Will Ushuddup
Apartment 609
44 Vaguerant Street
Despair
T5H 3R3

Rak Anwruin Properties Ltd.
89 Prophit Avenue
Despair
T5K 6W2

April 24, 1992

For the attention of Justin Itferabuk, President

INVOICE #001

For: Rental rebate for Apartment 609, from March 29 to
April 22, 1992, for failing to allow "peaceful possession
of the premises," through landlord installing unacceptably
noisy tenant in Apartment 709, on March 1, 1992.

Noise level persists for at least 45% of the time. Thus:

Monthly rent $875.00
45% of rent =   393.75

Amount due $393.75

Terms: Net monthly. Overdue accounts attract interest at
1.5% per month.

Such an ominous letter and invoice should convince the landlord that something must be done, and you will be able to settle the matter before actually having to give notice and move out.

If your demands are not complied with, and you decide to move, continue to send invoices every month until you do leave. If you really prefer to stay, and the landlord refuses to refund the 45%, include a statement with your second invoice, detailing the overdue $393.75, plus 1.5% interest of $5.90, plus current invoice of $393.75, and type prominently, "Unless this account is settled in full by Friday, June 5, 1992, a court summons will be filed without further notice," at the bottom of the page. If he still fails to respond, file the summons.

Should you decide to move, you should serve written notice of vacation as soon as you find new premises, giving the landlord as much time as possible to find a new tenant. If the notice is less than the legislated minimum requirement, then the reason must be included in your notice, as follows:

Apartment 609
44 Vaguerant Street
Despair
T5H 3R3

Rak Anwruin Properties Ltd.
89 Prophit Avenue
Despair
T5K 6W2

June 3, 1992

For the attention of Justin Itferabuk, President

Dear Mr. Itferabuk,

I shall be vacating the above apartment on June 30, 1992, against my will because of the disturbing and unacceptable noise levels that have deprived me of my legal entitlement to "peaceful possession of the premises" since March 1, 1992.

I remind you that numerous written and verbal complaints to you, your superintendent, and the tenant responsible for the noise have not met with any success in resolving the problem.

In the circumstances, I cannot be held responsible for the

amount of notice given, since my move is dictated by conditions outside my control. My moving expenses will be forwarded to your office for settlement.

Yours sincerely,

Will Ushuddup

c.c. Des Truktiv, tenant
    Ben Dovabakwodz, building superintendent

As soon as you are settled in your new apartment, send the invoice for all your moving expenses to the landlord. Remember to keep all the applicable receipts, as they may be needed later to verify the amount claimed. The invoice for the move should look something like this:

Will Ushuddup
Apartment 312
32 Haven Street
Despair
T4H 3S8

Rak Anwruin Properties Ltd.
89 Prophit Avenue
Despair
T5K 6W2

July 6, 1991

For the attention of Justin Itferabuk, President

INVOICE #004

Re: Apartment 609, 44 Vaguerant Street, Despair

For: Moving expenses, from above premises on June 30, 1992.

Mover charge $287.50

Connection fees, telephone, hydro,
cable television   83.34

Notifications of address change	38.00
Lost wages during moving	65.00
Difference between old and new rent (old rent $875.00/mo., new rent $918.00/mo.) 1 year lease = 12 X 43.00)	516.00
Total:	$989.84

Terms: Net monthly. Overdue accounts attract interest at 1.5% per month.

If none of the previously sent invoices have been paid, to save yourself the trouble of sending a final statement at a later date, you could give notice with this invoice that a summons will be filed for the total outstanding amount, unless full settlement is received by the end of the month.

There will always be a landlord somewhere who fails in his obligations and refuses to compensate tenants or correct any deficiencies that are his responsibility, no matter how hard the injured party pleads. In which case, a carefully recorded and correctly administered campaign to obtain satisfaction should receive favorable review in the courts.

HOTEL ROOM LACKS CLEANLINESS

The glossy brochures that advertise holidays tend to exaggerate the resorts they are trying to pitch. Pictures of golden beaches — deserted except for the perfectly tanned and scarcely attired model — blue skies, luxurious rooms, tables piled with delicacies, vintage wines, and exotic cocktails, as well as quaint local scenes are intended to lure travelers. However, reality does not always match these descriptions; you may find tiny littered beaches packed with people, hotels barely completed, adverse weather, and inedible food.

Of course, some variance from the descriptions can be expected, especially in the weather. Nonetheless, basic expectations must be met; the accommodation must be as close to the beach and amenities as advertised, the food should be palatable, and the hotel efficiently maintained and operated, and pleasant to stay in. If a particular service is intolerably substandard, what can you do to obtain an improvement? Complain, obviously. But how and when? And if the remedy is inadequate, how do you obtain compensation?

Assume you are vacationing overseas for two weeks. The trip is a package tour, booked in your hometown. When you arrive at your hotel, you notice immediately that your room is extremely dirty. The bathtub has rings around it, the cups are dirty, giant dust balls cover the floor under the bed, and the atmosphere is scarcely neutral! Since hotel rooms are typically cleaned most thoroughly in the time between when guests depart and new ones arrive, you are concerned the condition will only get worse.

So before you even unpack, you seek out the manager and ask him to accompany you back to your room, where you voice your indignation over the lack of cleanliness in such a way that translation will not be required even if language is a barrier. It is important to do this right away, since he will be more likely to respond to a new guest than to one who has already put up with things as they are for some days.

Do not unpack until the room has been cleaned to your satisfaction. If nothing is done within an acceptable period of time, find the manager again, and interrupt him no matter how busy he is elsewhere. If you are sufficiently indignant and persistent, he should quickly be persuaded that it is futile to ignore you. If he still dawdles, take your bags to the reception desk and continue your argument in public, where the commotion is sure to attract an audience. The manager will not be enthusiastic about having to defend his laxity in full view of other guests, diners, visitors, and staff, and he will probably act immediately to placate you. You might even take with you to the lobby a dirty cup, bag of dust balls, or filthy towel to create more impact. You will likely end up with the cleanest room in the hotel!

If this still does not produce the cleanliness you require, or if it is not maintained during the rest of your stay, you may want to seek damages from the tour operator when you get home. In order to justify any claim to which you may feel entitled, it is vital that you voice your complaints to the manager continually during your stay, at least once a day, in the hope that something may be done and that you have a record to show the tour operator that you did everything you could to obtain an improvement. Keep notes of the times you complained and to whom you spoke, what was promised, and what actual inconvenience you suffered. Determining how much to seek in compensation will be difficult, and will depend on how dirty the room actually was and to what degree it affected the enjoyment of your vacation.

Since you probably spent no more than two or three waking hours a day in the room during the vacation, you would probably not be entitled to a big percentage of the total cost of the trip. Nonetheless, the lack of cleanliness preyed on your mind, even when you were away from the hotel, and affected your enjoyment. You should seek a reasonable amount, one that does not make you appear greedy, yet high enough to prevent future problems for other tourists — ten to fifteen percent of the cost of the vacation might be in order. Once you have determined an amount, you will send a letter to the tour operator.

---

854 Spotless Lane
Nogermsin, Mysink
H6G 6Y3

Mann Ovabord Tours Ltd.
22 Flezenlice Street
Leftin, Ahury
T5Y 2S3

December 1, 1991

For the attention of Perry Grinate, President

Dear Mr. Grinate,

My wife and I have just returned from a two-week stay in the Hotel Sordide on the Costa Ransome, booked through your company as the enclosed copy of invoice will confirm.

I regret to inform you that our vacation was ruined by the appalling lack of hygiene practiced by the hotel, which, despite our combined daily efforts itemized on the enclosed list, continued to plague us until the day we left. This is the first time I have had occasion to complain to your otherwise excellent company, and I have no doubt an organization with your reputation will want to launch an immediate investigation into the operation of this hotel so that future clients will not have to endure a similar unpleasant experience.

I am sure you will want to offer compensation for our grossly inadequate accommodation, per enclosed list of complaints and invoice for what I hope you will agree is a reasonable rebate under the circumstances.

Please let me have your observations with the remittance, as well as your assurances that our experience will not be repeated on future excursions with your organization.

Thank you in anticipation.

Yours sincerely,

Drew A. Blanc

Encls.

The letter confirms that you are a regular client, and that you will continue to patronize the tour operator if you are compensated at the requested amount. Enclose your invoice thus:

Mr. & Mrs. Drew A. Blanc
854 Spotless Lane
Nogermsin, Mysink
H6G 6Y3

Mann Ovabord Tours Ltd.
22 Flezenlice Street
Leftin, Ahury
T5Y 2S3

December 1, 1991

For the attention of Perry Grinate, President

INVOICE #01-91

Re: Vacation for two persons, 14 days/nights at Hotel Sordide, Costa Ransome, your reference HS/56456

Total amount paid $3,456.00

Compensation required for suffering due to grossly inadequate hygienic conditions at hotel, detailed on separate enclosed list.

$345.60

Terms: net monthly

Also enclose the list of your complaints and your attempts to have them rectified, and what results your efforts produced, something like this:

Tour #HS/56456 Hotel Sordide, Costa Ransome

List of Complaints

November 17. Arrived at hotel. Complained three times to manager, Mr. Idi Otte, about filthy toilet, cockroaches, litter, dirty sheets, no light bulb in bedroom. Nothing was done.

November 18. Complained four times to manager, and three times to receptionist. Room still has filthy toilet, cockroaches, litter, dirty sheets, no light bulb in bedroom. Still nothing was done. (And so on.)

By the time you have covered fourteen days' worth of inconvenience, the list will look most impressive, and should evoke ready sympathy and a refund from the tour operator.

Most tour companies will listen to their customers and will want to satisfy reasonable complaints. If you are dealing with a company of doubtful repute, and they are not willing to see your point of view, then a more strongly worded letter may be required.

---

854 Spotless Lane
Nogermsin, Mysink
H6G 6Y3

Mann Ovabord Tours Ltd.
22 Flezenlice Street
Leftin, Ahury
T5Y 2S3

December 7, 1991

For the attention of Perry Grinate, President

Dear Mr. Grinate,

I am in receipt of your letter dated December 6, and I am sorry to read that you do not appear to consider your company responsible for the inadequacy of hotels provided for your clients. I am quite unable to accept the contents of your letter, and hold you fully liable for the suffering my wife and I experienced through your failure to monitor the facilities offered by Hotel Sordide.

Kindly, therefore, be aware that unless my invoice for $345.60 is settled in full by Wednesday, December 18, 1991, a summons will be filed without further notice.

Yours sincerely,

Drew A. Blanc

c.c. Hon. Dick Tayter, Minister of Consumer
      and Commercial Relations
    Ellie Fant, President, Alliance of National Travel
      Associations
    Hugo Farr, President, Fluds, Fammin, & Pestilants
      Travel Agents Ltd.

Send copies of the complete correspondence to the authority that handles travel complaints, the Travel Association, and the agency where you booked the vacation. They should encourage Mann Ovabord to settle your bill.

If not, then you should file as promised. Your chances of a favorable judgment should be excellent.

Had you booked your own accommodations separately, things would have been much simpler. You would have demanded that your deposit, if there was one, be returned and then left to seek a hotel elsewhere. Or if they refused to refund your deposit, you could have stayed until the deposit amount had been covered and then checked out. Or, if there was no alternative hotel, you could have stayed for the duration, and paid the bill less an amount for the uncleanliness, documented of course by the detailed account of your woes.

9

Fear of Flying: Taking on the Airlines

Although advertisements regularly proclaim that airlines provide trouble-free travel to their passengers, problems can and do arise.

OVERBOOKED FLIGHT

Airlines routinely overbook flights to compensate for "no-shows" — the passengers who book a flight and don't show up. If the predicted number of overbooked passengers don't appear, the airline is relieved that it can indeed accommodate all the passengers who do. Occasionally, however, the system backfires — the no-shows show up — and the airline must "bump" passengers off the flight. The normal bumping procedure is for the airline in question to ask for volunteers who are willing to stand down in exchange for compensation, which varies from one company to another. If too few volunteer, then the airline may select passengers to stay behind against their wishes. Passengers flying during peak travel periods may be especially at risk.

If you are unlucky enough to be bumped against your wishes, you need not accept whatever compensation the airline offers you, even if the airline tries to convince you that the compensation they offer is standard for the circumstances, and is not negotiable. Fellow passengers may accept the airline's offer, but you do not have to comply just because they have. Whatever the purpose of your trip, be it holiday or business, you are entitled to claim damages. But since you have yet to depart for your destination, you are not in a position to know the amount of inconvenience the delay is going to cause, so negotiating compensation is extremely premature, rather like negotiating a divorce settlement during a wedding ceremony!

Imagine that you and your spouse are looking forward to a long-overdue and well-deserved two-week holiday in Tenerife. You have survived the frenzied last-minute packing, the mad dash to the airport, and the seemingly endless wait at the check-in counter, and you are both now in the departure lounge eagerly awaiting your departure to a warmer climate. By noon local time to-morrow, Thursday, you should be lounging on the beach.

Suddenly, an announcement informs the expectant gathering that, due to unfortunate circumstances, there are insufficient seats to accommodate the number of passengers booked on this particular flight. The message offers profuse apologies, and requests that eight passengers volunteer to wait for the next flight. A few minutes later, there is a request for more volunteers, since only four travelers have decided to accept a delay in their schedule. Soon after, the crackled voice names four people who are to report to the boarding repre-sentative. Your names are among the four.

With mounting apprehension, you approach the desk, where the represen-tative informs you, again with profuse apologies, that since you were among the last passengers to book this flight, you will have to step down and take the next available flight. Your protests are greeted with sympathy, but the decision is final, and you are given no choice but to resign yourselves to your fate.

You are guaranteed a reservation on the next flight, which is at 3:30 p.m. tomorrow, which means you won't arrive in Tenerife until early Friday. The airline offers to accommodate you at their expense in a nearby hotel, includ-ing $50.00 each for meals and incidentals, and free transportation to the hotel and back. If this suits your immediate requirements, go ahead and accept the airline's offer, but make quite sure the representative understands that your acceptance is not to be interpreted as full settlement and that you will be submitting a claim when you return from Tenerife in two weeks.

Do not sign any standard documentation that may impede your right to seek further damages. If the airline insists that you sign a waiver in order to qualify for the compensation, you should refuse to do so. You will instead organize your own overnight lodging, and add it to the final bill upon your return. In this case, however, the company has bowed to your insistence, filed the waiver unsigned, and you go to your temporary lodging.

The next day all goes smoothly: you make it to the airport on time, the flight leaves on schedule, the stopover in Madrid is short, and you finally ar-rive at your Tenerife hotel in time for a continental breakfast on the patio of your hotel. After two weeks away from it all, you arrive home, and it is time to consider your claim against the airline.

You still had to pay the hotel in Tenerife for the missed first night, which, since it was booked separately from your flight, is easy to calculate. In order to catch the missed flight, you lost three hours' wages, and your spouse, a nurse who normally works the night shift, lost eight hours' pay — again straightforward. And you lost vacation time, which is not as easy to put a dollar value on. But you decide to claim for the cost of a day's accommodation and meals. Once you have determined the amount of your claim, send a statement of your account as follows:

---

747 Beach Avenue
Iskapism
H4G 2M7

Fryteflite Airlines Inc.
Hijaque Building
Zepallin
F4G 8K3

April 20, 1992

For the attention of Bud Jerigar, President

Dear Mr. Jerigar,

On Wednesday, April 1, 1992, at approximately 3:30 p.m., my wife and I deposited our luggage with your check-in desk at Chambels Airport, and made our way to the departure lounge, where we confidently waited to board your flight number FF 786, scheduled to leave for Tenerife at 4:30 p.m. To our astonishment and dismay, thirty minutes before our intended flight, we were told by your airport representative, a Miss Emma Jency, that our reservation would not be honored because your company had accepted bookings in excess of the number of seats available. Despite our protests at this unexpected and appalling treatment, we were forced to take a flight the next day.

Apart from the disruption and shortening of our eagerly awaited vacation, we both lost wages in order to make it to the airport only to find that the departure dates specified on your tickets were meaningless. We had to spend an unwanted night in an airport hotel. When we finally arrived at our destination, we found that your disgraceful performance had ruined the mood of our vacation.

I hold your organization entirely responsible for the
losses we have incurred through your negligence,
and enclose our invoice for immediate
settlement.

Yours sincerely,

Phil Ourpursiz

Encl.

The invoice accompanying the letter should look something like this:

                                        Phil and Lyne Ourpursiz
                                        747 Beach Avenue
                                        Iskapism
                                        H4G 2M7

Fryteflite Airlines Inc.
Hijaque Building
Zepallin
F4G 8K3

                                        April 20, 1992

INVOICE

For expenses and inconvenience suffered through denial
of boarding flight number FF 786 on April 1, 1992.

Lost wages:

Phil Ourpursiz, 3 hours
April 1 (2:00 to 5:00 p.m) at $18.25 per hour $54.75

Lyne Ourpursiz, 8 hours nursing shift
April 1-2 (8:00 p.m. to 4:00 a.m) at
$16.73 per hour   133.84

Loss of 1 day hotel accommodation and meals

in Tenerife. (Total cost of 14 days/nights
$1,820.00) 130.00   130.00

Loss of enjoyment and disruption
of vacation   250.00

                              TOTAL $568.59

Terms: Check by return mail

Overdue accounts attract interest at 1.5% per month.

Most airlines will settle expenses that have been inflicted through their deliberate policy of overselling aircraft seats. After all, this policy resulted in a full payload on your original flight, and the amount you are claiming in compensation is less than the price of a single return fare.

However, if the airline dithers, a further prod might expedite matters. Write something along these lines:

---

747 Beach Avenue
Iskapism
H4G 2M7

Fryteflite Airlines Inc.
Hijaque Building
Zepallin
F4G 8K3

April 27, 1992

For the attention of Al Battros, Chairman

Dear Mr. Battros,

My letter and account of April 20, addressed personally
for the attention of your president, Mr. Bud Jerigar,
has yet to be afforded the courtesy of a reply.

I am sure you will agree that the matter demands
immediate attention, and I therefore trust you will take

urgent steps to ensure that the matter is resolved without
further delay.

I look forward to your early settlement, and thank you in
anticipation.

Yours sincerely,

Phil Ourpursiz

c.c. Bud Jerigar, President

The copy to the president will warn him that the chairman is about to inquire
why his valuable time has been imposed upon for a trifling claim of $568.59!
As usual, you have given few details so that the chairman will be forced to
find out what is going on. Your persistence should result in a quick settlement, but if not, another letter is in order.

---

747 Beach Avenue
Iskapism
H4G 2M7

Fryteflyte Airlines Inc.
Hijaque Building
Zepallin
F4G 8K3

May 4, 1992

For the attention of Bud Jerigar, President

Dear Mr. Jerigar,

I have received your letter dated May 1, 1992,
confirming that your company is concerned only
with making as much profit as possible, with no
interest or consideration for your unfortunate
passengers.

Unless my account for $568.59 is settled in full by

Tuesday, May 19, 1992, a court summons will be filed without further notice.

Yours sincerely,

Phil Ourpursiz

c.c. Al Battros, Chairman

It is unlikely that the airline will want to risk unnecessary bad publicity, particularly since their chances of winning in court are slim. Fortunately, most reputable airlines will capitulate well before threats of legal action become necessary.

YOU ARRIVE — BUT YOUR SUITCASE DOESN'T

When you check your baggage in at the airport, invariably you wonder, if only subconsciously, whether you will ever see it again. Happily, the majority of suitcases do get on the same flight as their owners, or if they go astray, the airlines usually find them within a day or so, and return them safely to their anxious owners.

Some precautions will help ensure that your luggage arrives when you do:

- Avoid using expensive luggage, especially if traveling in poor countries — thieves may be eager to discover whether the contents are equally opulent.
- Make sure your luggage is sound, because it may be subject to vigorous treatment on its journey, and a defective suitcase may not last the trip.
- Remove all old labels and tags to avoid confusing baggage handlers. Check-in attendants usually do this as a matter of routine, but you should make sure the job has been done before your bags disappear down the conveyor belt.
- Don't check in at the last minute — your bag may not make it on board, even if you do. In which case, you can only hope that the airline will be good enough to send it on the next flight. If the baggage is subsequently lost, any claim that you might have for compensation may be less than watertight.

If you take all these precautions, your luggage may arrive when you do! If, despite these precautions, your luggage is lost, then the airline will have to provide compensation.

Most airlines have a fixed compensation schedule for such loss, which varies from company to company, and which may not cover your losses. Such guidelines do not have to be taken at face value, however, and passengers should be entitled to the cost of replacing their property and any other losses that were suffered as a consequence.

Say your suitcase fails to arrive on the carousel after your flight. All the other passengers have collected their bags and departed. You find a representative of the airline and report the loss immediately. They will have a standard procedure for tracing anything that has been misplaced, and there is not much else that you can do other than leave the matter in their hands. After you have supplied all the details required, take the name and telephone number of the representative, who will in turn have recorded the address and telephone number of your destination.

You should ask whether the luggage will be sent to you as soon as it is located, or whether you will be expected to collect it. If you are told that you will have to return to the airport to collect it, make it clear that your travel expenses in doing so will be the responsibility of the airline, in which case they may decide they would prefer to deliver it instead!

Point out that you will need certain items that were in your suitcase immediately, and the longer you are without it, the more replacements you will be obliged to purchase or rent. Leave no doubt that all your expenses will have to be covered by the airline, which will give them the option of supplying you with some of the items you require, or suggesting where they may prefer you to make any purchases or rentals.

Whether your luggage has been temporarily misplaced or permanently lost, try to do what is most reasonable and appropriate for both parties, without inconveniencing yourself unduly. Say you are on a skiing trip, for instance, and you naturally expect to venture onto the slopes first thing tomorrow morning. It would hardly be interpreted as fair and reasonable if you purchased brand-new equipment, when quite adequate substitutes can be rented just as easily. Your own luggage might arrive safely at the end of the first day's stay, so renting rather than buying should be the preferred option for most items, unless you know for certain that your cases have been lost or stolen.

The airline will do its best to locate your missing luggage, and your cooperation is necessary to reinforce your subsequent claim with sound evidence of goodwill. Before you rent or purchase an expensive item, for instance, call the representative to check whether the airline has succeeded in finding your baggage, and to see if they have any suggestions as to the most expedient way of obtaining your latest requirement.

Maintaining a log of all your attempts to keep your (their) expenses to a minimum will greatly enhance the chances of your settling your claim without serious contest. Keep all receipts, including those for transportation to and from rental companies or retailers where you had to obtain replacements. When you have completed your vacation or business trip, type up a list of your expenses, and send it in the form of an invoice, with a covering letter to the airline, as follows:

---

23 Frateloss Avenue
Pillferring
R3T 3U8

Pan Demonium Airlines
1 Kramptseetz Place
Jettlagd
H5C 9L2

December 4, 1991

For the attention of Bau Ingg, President

Dear Mr. Ingg,

The enjoyment of my annual ski trip last month to Kraktribbs Mountain Resort received a severe setback when my baggage was inadvertently sent to San Taklaus by Pan Demonium Airlines instead of accompanying me on flight PD328 to Ruttd Tarmaak Airport, on November 17.

I had to wait four days, until the evening of November 21, for my suitcases to be retrieved and returned to me, which as you may imagine, was extremely irksome and inconvenient, particularly since I was carrying new and expensive skiing equipment.

During this time, although I managed as best I could without several personal effects, I was obliged to rent or buy some essentials to tide me over, as discussed on each occasion with your very helpful representative at Ruttd Tarmaak, Ms. Helen Hiwater. This is the first time I have ever been parted from my luggage in many years of

flying, and I am surprised that it happened on one of
your flights, for I have always found your service to be
very efficient and competitive.

I enclose my bill for the expenses incurred as a result of
this unfortunate incident, and as I am sure you will agree, I
have succeeded in keeping unavoidable expenditures to an
absolute minimum, considering the circumstances. Your
early settlement will be greatly appreciated.

Yours sincerely,

Lisa Pearovskeez

Encl.

Enclose copies of the receipts and keep the originals. The airline is entirely at
fault for losing your luggage; your letter has shown that you are a regular flier
who prefers to travel with Pan Demonium, and your invoice shows that you
kept costs to a minimum. This combination should ensure that early reimbursement will be made.

In the unlikely event your claim is disputed, drop a line to the chairman as
follows:

---

23 Frateloss Avenue
Pillferring
R3T 3U8

Pan Demonium Airlines
1 Kramptseetz Place
Jettlagd
H5C 9L2

December 8, 1991

For the attention of Roy Alairforss, Chairman

Dear Mr. Alairforss,

I am in receipt of a letter from your president, Mr. Bau
Ingg, which informs me that Pan Demonium Airlines does

not accept responsibility for expenses incurred by
passengers when their possessions are lost through
mishandling by your baggage handlers.

I would be greatly obliged if you could confirm that Mr.
Ingg has misinterpreted company policy toward those
unfortunate enough to suffer losses for which your airline
is entirely liable.

Perhaps you would also be kind enough to inform Mr.
Ingg that unless my invoice dated December 4, for
$471.50, is paid in full by Monday, December 23, 1991,
a summons will be filed without further notice.

Yours sincerely,

Lisa Pearovskeez

c.c. Bau Ingg, President

It is doubtful that the airline will want to risk going to court and losing a case
in which they have no defense and that may attract adverse publicity. A check
should therefore soon be on its way.

If Pan Demonium persists in denying your claim, then file the summons as
promised. This will convince them that you are serious, and mean to be paid.
They will probably settle before a court appearance becomes necessary.

10

If All Else Fails

The principal purpose of this book is to show you how to settle claims through written communication. Occasionally, however, you may have no alternative but to take your case to court.

SMALL CLAIMS COURT

If your claim is not excessive — from $500 to $3,000, depending on prevailing limits in your area — it can be heard in small claims court. You can verify the small claims limits in your area by calling your local court, listed in the blue, or government, pages of your telephone directory.

Small claims court is an uncomplicated arbitration vehicle for people or businesses that may not have much legal experience. Filing a claim is simple; you do not need a lawyer to act on your behalf.

I strongly recommend that you attend a court session as an interested spectator. This valuable experience will give you the confidence to appear in court yourself should it become necessary. Your local court can give you information regarding times. Try to arrive before a session begins, while the "players" are still shuffling around and glaring at one another! There are usually several sessions going on at once, so if a case is boring, you can go to another courtroom.

You will be pleasantly surprised and reassured to see that the judges wear everyday clothes. Small claims court judges conduct hearings in plain English, and there is no jury. There are no vicious and articulate high-profile lawyers intimidating witnesses and defendants into terrified submission. In fact, appearances by lawyers are rare; if a party does have a lawyer, the judge will often intervene if the lawyer uses legal terminology to baffle or intimidate those who do not enjoy the same access or training. The court is there to arbitrate a fair solution to disputes, not to hold auditions for budding Perry Masons.

A claim must usually be filed in the appropriate court for the district in which the claim arose or the one nearest to the address of the defendant. To file a claim, you must obtain the correct form from the court. The form is straightforward, usually just one page. If you need help in filling it out, call the court for advice. The clerks are used to answering questions from ordinary citizens and will be pleased to help you; you will not be sneered at or told to get a lawyer.

You, as the claimant, are the plaintiff, and the opposition is the defendant(s). In the appropriate areas, you must provide both your and the defendant's name, address, and telephone number. Next, fill in the amount and nature of the claim — damage to property, unpaid account, etc. Finally, there is a large section in which you can provide details of the claim. If you have been diligent about keeping records, notes, and copies of correspondence, you can attach copies to your claim along with any other relevant evidence. Once you have finished filling out the form, sign it and take it to the court, where a clerk will make sure you have completed all the sections and relieve you of the filing fee, which is usually between $25 and $50, depending on the amount of the claim. The fee is added to the claim, so that if you win the case, the fee will be returned to you. The court then processes the claim, and serves the defendant(s) with a summons.

Serving a summons can take between a week and three months, depending on how it is served — by hand or by mail — and how busy the court is. Once it has been served, the court will inform you of the defendant's response. If the claim is not disputed, the defendant will pay the full amount, including the filing fee, into the court. When the check has been cleared, the court will in turn remit a check to you in full settlement.

If the defendant does not file a defense within the allotted time, usually twenty days, you can file a judgment. This means that the defendant cannot contest your claim and will have to settle. If he does not do so, you can instruct the court to issue a garnishment, which is attached to the wages or bank account of the defendant. If this is not possible, the court can issue a writ of seizure and sale against the defendant's property, for the amount of the claim, or a summons for the defendant to appear before a judge. These procedures can all be set in motion in the court office, and the court clerk will be happy to help you complete the necessary forms.

However, if the defendant files a defense, the court will send you a copy and notify you of the time and date of the trial. If you require any witnesses to speak on your behalf or you wish to cross-examine them before the judge, you should instruct the court to issue a subpoena, which is a writ commanding the person named on it to appear at a legal proceeding. You can subpoena as many witnesses as you think are needed for your case.

A defendant can still settle before the case goes to trial. The prospect of sitting around in a small claims court for hours over a relatively small amount of money, with the risk of losing the case at the end of the day, may induce the defendant to capitulate. However, if a pretrial settlement is not forthcoming, then you must prepare yourself and your evidence for the hearing.

You do not need to prepare long speeches filled with the brilliant legal terminology heard on *Street Legal* and *L.A. Law*, and the judge will not want to hear you repeat everything in your claim. Instead, prepare a list of pertinent questions you want to ask the defendant or witnesses, as well as notes of any other information you feel is relevant to the case. The judge will probably have studied your case before his session, and if the evidence you have submitted is clear and comprehensive, he may be close to making a decision before he hears either side address the court. This does not mean that he has prejudged your case; there may be points he will want clarified. Concentrate on confirming and reinforcing evidence rather than duplicating it.

On the day of the hearing, make sure you arrive in good time, and let the court clerk know you are in attendance. Be sure to bring along absolutely everything you might need that relates to the case. Dress neatly and conservatively — first impressions are important, and no matter how impartial a judge is supposed to be, he is human and therefore more apt to sympathize with you if you look like someone with whom he might socialize. And don't try to be amusing; it is the judge who is holding court, not you. Just be brief and to the point — the judge has heard it all before, and he just wants facts and straight answers to his questions. The quicker he can settle the case, the happier he will be.

During the proceedings, try to stay calm, even if you are being maligned by the opposition. Don't raise your voice, don't interrupt anyone, and don't call anyone a liar. Use positive terminology to argue a point; saying that "the defendant's claim . . . appears to contradict what actually happened," will do far more for your credibility than saying, "That's absolute garbage, you lying moron!" Don't try to emulate your favorite television lawyer. Amateur histrionics will not impress the judge. He knows you are not a lawyer and does not expect you to behave like one. You are a wronged citizen putting his or her faith in the wisdom and experience of the learned judge. Your actions and words should demonstrate this.

You should address the judge as "Your Honor" when he speaks to you, and never reply to his questions until he has finished speaking. As you will have observed if you took the time to sit in on a few cases before you initiated your claim, judges are easily irritated, and the smallest annoyance can incur their displeasure, particularly if the session is a long one. A lot of cases are conducted in a disorganized fashion, and the judge's patience is often sorely tried. After the judge has finished speaking to you, or has given you some advice or information, show your appreciation with a simple "Thank you, Your Honor."

This sounds like an obvious courtesy, but it is rarely exercised. And a little flattery can be advantageous.

If the defendant has a lawyer, and during cross-examination he or she uses terminology you do not understand, or attempts to bully you into admitting something that is not true, stay calm, apologize to the judge, and ask him to explain it to you. He will be pleased to demonstrate his prowess as an interpreter and will enjoy the opportunity to instruct the offending lawyer in the art of using language that can be readily understood by mere mortals. Few judges will turn down an opportunity to show the congregation that they are completely in charge, and if this includes chastising an overzealous lawyer, so much the better.

When all the evidence has been presented, and the cross-examinations concluded, both parties are usually asked to make a brief statement, or summary, of the main points of their respective arguments, after which the judge will sum up. Usually he will then make his decision, which is binding, and you are free to go. Occasionally, if a case is complicated, he may reserve judgment for a few days, perhaps while he ponders a legal point, and you will be notified of his decision by mail. If judgment is in your favor, the defendant will be required to pay the money into court, and it will then be sent to you after due process.

If the amount you are suing for exceeds the maximum permitted by small claims court, you will have to file your claim with a higher court — district or county court, whichever applies in your area. The procedures will be similar to those outlined above for small claims, but there are differences, and the potential for complications that may require legal advice is far greater. The higher court, for example, will not provide the plaintiff with a claim form; one will have to be purchased from a legal stationer.

It is certainly possible to proceed without a lawyer. However, you may risk losing your case because you don't have the legal expertise to present your case skillfully. If the amount you are suing for is substantial, the defendant will probably have experienced counsel, and you will be ill-equipped to handle the tricks he will throw your way. The court will be more formal, and the judge less tolerant of a litigant who is out of his depth. Furthermore, he is unlikely to admonish a lawyer who uses terminology you find obscure, and may be content to "let the best man win." Unfortunately, you may not be aware of the strength of the opposing lawyer until the hearing is in session, and this is no time to discover that you are hopelessly outclassed. You would be well advised, therefore, to seek some legal advice.

SELECTING GOOD COUNSEL

Finding a competent lawyer who has sound experience in your particular type of claim can be a surprisingly difficult task. If you do not know a lawyer or have never used one before, you risk selecting one for all the wrong reasons.

You can of course find lawyers listed in the yellow pages of your directory. But how do you choose the right one for you? Lawyers' names and phone numbers say nothing about their competence. And ads luring clients with vague promises are no help either. A "free initial consultation" may be a genuine and generous offer by a highly competent lawyer who is setting up a new practice, or it may indicate a bad lawyer who has to offer incentives to drum up business. "Fees you can live with" may in fact send you into instant bankruptcy, but you would presumably still be alive to enjoy the experience! The yellow pages, then, are not the best place to look for a lawyer.

If your best friend is a legal secretary, she might be able to put you in touch with someone suitable. But she will likely recommend the lawyers who work for her firm out of loyalty to her employers, which is not much better than using the yellow pages.

Court clerks may be able to help you; after all, they spend their days dealing with lawyers and watching them in action. Their opinion could be useful, but remember that they may be biased against certain lawyers, particularly ones who don't treat clerks with the respect with which they would like to be accustomed.

Would it be worth contacting a "celebrity" lawyer, one whose name is regularly in the news or who writes books or columns? Probably not. Their fees, which will have risen to reflect their elevated status in the community, will likely be prohibitive, and some lawyer-authors may not have time for serious practice anymore.

Your best option is to get referrals from friends or colleagues whose judgment you can rely on. Or you can contact a legal referral center, if there is one in your community. Even then there may be pitfalls.

Lawyers have different strengths and specializations; a real estate lawyer, for example, may not have the knowledge to successfully prosecute a claim for personal injury in an automobile accident. So try to ascertain the strengths of the lawyers recommended to you, and whether they have successfully handled cases like yours. You could find someone who had what appeared to be an iron-clad case, which was entrusted to experienced and proven counsel, but was beaten, despite all efforts, by the defendant's lawyer. You then ascertain the name of the victor, and offer him or her your brief!

When you find someone who appears competent and experienced in your type of claim, make an appointment to discuss the case in detail and a mutually agreeable fee structure. Make a list of all the questions you need answered before the meeting, leaving space for the answers, so there are no doubts or gray areas after you leave the office. Feel free to ask anything you think important; you will not want any unexpected surprises when the case is well under way. There is no reason that reputable lawyers shouldn't welcome a potential client's interest in their modus operandi, and if they are evasive or vague, then you should probably take your business elsewhere.

You should be clear from the outset what the legal fees will be, and how they are calculated — some lawyers have fixed prices for certain services, or they may charge an hourly rate, which is applied to every bit of time the lawyer or his assistants work on your case, including research and filing documents. Even telephone conversations may be timed for billing.

You should inquire about your chances for success, how long the proceedings are expected to take, whether there is a chance to settle out of court, and so on. Will the lawyer accept calls at home, or only during office hours? Does she spend a lot of time in court, honing her skills? Will she handle the case herself, or will part of it be looked after by a junior colleague? Will she adhere rigidly to your wishes, and seek permission to deviate? Will she keep you up to date on all developments?

If you are satisfied on all fronts, then you can verbally inform the lawyer you will be pleased to have him or her act on your behalf, and confirm all the details in writing, including your understanding of the terms and conditions you discussed. Write something along these lines:

---

36 Planetiv Avenue
Casty Gate
F3G 9R2

Willie Lynchem
Wrritt, Harras, Flogg, & Lynchem, Solicitors
Gibbet Towers
Brybeville
W4L 8N9

March 4, 1992

Dear Mr. Lynchem,

Further to our pleasant meeting this morning, I enclose all details of my claim against the International Kolerah Hotel, which you have kindly agreed to conduct on my behalf.

I have noted for my records your fees of $83.00 per hour, which will be billed to me on a weekly basis, and that you anticipate complete recovery of my costs from the defendants, in the event of our winning the trial. I understand that you will keep me informed of events as they transpire, and consult with me as often as necessary. Should a compromise be desirable, in your opinion, I understand you will fully acquaint me with the details and reasons, <u>prior</u> to any agreement with defendants or their counsel.

Please let me know if I can offer you any further information. I look forward to your regular reports that this case is proceeding to an early and successful conclusion.

Best regards.

Yours sincerely,

Wilf Uldamige

Encls.

Your letter confirms exactly what your expectations are, and reminds him that you are not abandoning the case to his discretion and that you intend to keep fully abreast of his progress.

Make sure things get under way as soon as possible, and check with your lawyer as necessary to ensure that the momentum does not slacken off. Don't become a nuisance, with daily calls at inconvenient times. A few regular calls at appropriate stages will do.

When discussing any strategy or point that requires your decision, make sure you fully understand the lawyer's explanation of the subject. If the terminology is obscure legalese, get him to translate the information into layman's terms.

You should also do your part — keep your lawyer informed of any developments he may not be aware of, let him know if you expect to be away for more than a few days, let him handle the case as discussed, and pay your bills as agreed. Providing you maintain a good working relationship, you should be able to pursue your claim to a satisfactory conclusion.

11

The Author Is Put to the Test!

In November 1989, I was finally persuaded to succumb to the attractions of electronic technology, and so, suitably anesthetized for the ordeal, I ventured in the direction of a computer store, where the entire contents of my wallet was painlessly exchanged for the latest in high-tech wizardry! The reason I made this rash and untypical expenditure was to give my ancient manual typewriter a well-deserved retirement, and to make the writing of this book a more comfortable and efficient experience.

This was the first computer I had ever used, let alone owned, and I consequently treated it with every possible consideration, to ensure any malfunction would not be the result of mistreatment on my part. The components were carefully unpacked and assembled in a temperate and stable area, grounded immediately, and no drink or foodstuff was ever allowed near the work area. In fact, I used it infrequently until the beginning of 1991.

I was, therefore, surprised and concerned when, in February 1991, the monitor began to malfunction on occasion; the screen would black out for a few seconds or minutes, recover, and then continue to operate normally. Since I had no idea whether this was an indication that something was amiss, or whether computers were prone to the occasional cough or stutter, I called the store that had sold it to me for an opinion. The service manager was most helpful and knowledgeable, and informed me immediately that the power supply was probably failing, and that I could expect the problem to worsen and the computer to expire sooner or later.

I expressed surprise at this premature failure, and explained that the unit had experienced very little use since its purchase. Could I therefore expect it to be repaired at the expense of the manufacturer? I asked.

The inevitable answer was that the one-year warranty had expired, and that I would have to pay for the repair myself. The manager was sympathetic, but explained that he was obliged to adhere to the warranty conditions imposed by the manufacturer. I informed him that although I appreciated his position, I was not impressed by the performance of my machine, and would be writing to the makers to discover whether they would be prepared to consider my grievance. The manager wished me luck, but warned me that in his long and varied experience with this manufacturer, they had always adhered rigidly to warranty conditions, and that my chances of obtaining satisfaction were very slim indeed. I then sent the following letter to the manufacturer:

---

2 Bloor Street West
Suite 100
Toronto, Ontario
M4W 3E2

Lemon Computers Inc.
5342 Servis Road
Terminal Corners
H4J 8S3

April 2, 1991

For the attention of Mike Wrochipp, President

Dear Mr. Wrochipp,

On the advice of my publisher, Stoddart Publishing, I purchased a Cardigan GT from the University of Whizdom Computer Shop, on November 17, 1989, in order to expedite the completion of my latest book.

Although, as matters transpired, I didn't seriously start the book until the beginning of February this year, I did use my computer to type the occasional letter and invoice in the interim, and there is no doubt that I am enormously impressed with its capabilities.

However, on February 26 this year, the monitor started to black out occasionally, and I called the service manager of the computer store, who diagnosed the problem to be a failing power supply. The screen still blacks out for a few minutes every few days, but thus far I have not taken any steps to repair it. I am told that the repair would not be covered by warranty, since the unit is more than a year old. However, since, by my calculation it has been used for only 150 to 200 hours from new, and it has not been moved or mistreated in any way, this must be a fault that occurs more readily than one might suppose, and is therefore qualified under a further warranty.

My assumption is based on the premise that under normal commercial use, my 200 hours would be reached after only five weeks, which would be covered by the regular warranty.

I should very much appreciate hearing that you are able to authorize the necessary repair at no cost to myself, under the circumstances. The serial number is S34987658765378, and if you wish to send a representative to confirm the condition and slight usage of the unit, please let me know.

Thank you in anticipation.

Yours sincerely,

Bruce West

The letter was duly dispatched, and while I waited for a response, I called a friend of mine, a computer engineer who used to work for the company that manufactured my machine. He confirmed that it did sound as if the power supply was at fault. However, since he had not worked for that manufacturer for some time, he did not know whether this particular model was prone to unreliability. He was able to confirm that my chances of getting the warranty extended were very remote. Not very encouraging news.

But, as a starving author engaged in the very act of describing the most expedient procedures for combatting unfair trading practices, I knew that if I failed to pursue this one to a satisfactory resolution, I would never be able to look myself in the monitor again!

Then, on April 5, before I had received any acknowledgment or reply to my letter, the monitor suddenly blacked out permanently, and I was obliged to take it back to the computer store. They were able to confirm that the power supply needed replacing, and I left the unit for repair. Unfortunately, after it was repaired, collected and paid for, it didn't work at all, and I had to go back yet again to have a loose cable tightened! As soon as this additional service had been performed, all was happily back to normal.

A reply to my letter finally arrived on April 16, from the "acting president," who, as accurately predicted by my two advisers, informed me that "we will have to decline your request for a warranty extension."

Among the numerous reasons for refusing liability was this intriguing sentence: "Computers can be affected by many outside causes such as electrostatic discharge (static electricity received from walking across a carpet), electrical storms, radio frequency interference, power surges or dips, and other inconspicuous events."

I carefully resisted the temptation to point out that, to the best of my knowledge, my computer had not yet fully mastered the art of "walking across a carpet," and replied as follows:

---

2 Bloor Street West
Suite 100
Toronto, Ontario
M4W 3E2

Lemon Computers Inc.
5342 Servis Road
Terminal Corners
H4J 8S3

April 18, 1991

For the attention of Mike Wrochipp, President

Dear Mr. Wrochipp,

Further to my letter of April 2, regarding my Cardigan GT serial no. S34987658765378, the power supply failed completely on April 5, and was replaced at the University of Whizdom Computer Shop. When I arrived home with the repaired unit, it would not work at all, and I had to take it back again the following Monday, April 8, where the very helpful engineer diagnosed a cable that was not properly connected. He informed me that the cable had "crept" under expansion and contraction, and had thus disconnected itself, and that this was not an uncommon problem.

I am, incidentally, in receipt of a letter from your Mr. Hans Uporichute, the second paragraph of which suggests several circumstances as possible reasons for the premature failure of my machine. My machine has not been subjected to any of the stated events, and even if it had, the power supply is the most robust part of a system unit and would not have been affected. Any properly designed power supply should last indefinitely, which suggests that the Cardigan GT suffers from a generic fault.

Perhaps Mr. Uporichute would be good enough to confirm that none of the mishaps he listed could have been inflicted on my unit during its 10,060-mile journey from your factory in Singapore to Toronto, prior to my purchasing it. I see no validity in your argument, and enclose my invoice for the expenses and inconvenience that I have suffered through your faulty product.

Yours sincerely,

Bruce West

Encls.

The invoice accompanying the letter included a photocopy of the work order and paid invoice from the computer shop.

Bruce West
2 Bloor Street West
Suite 100
Toronto, Ontario
M4W 3E2

Lemon Computers Inc.
5342 Servis Road
Terminal Corners
H4J 8S3

April 18, 1991

For the attention of Mike Wrochipp, President

INVOICE NO. 2121/91

For repair to Cardigan GT No. S34987658765378,
premature failure of power supply $185.50

Transportation to and from repair shop, correspondence, etc.		53.70
Loss of time (two and a half days) during repair, nominal amount		50.00
	Total	$289.20

Terms: Check by return post.

Overdue accounts attract interest at 1.5% per month.

The letter and invoice were sent the same day, and I anticipated an interesting response to my latest riposte!

This came, unexpectedly, and in the form of a telephone call, from a young lady at the office of the manufacturer, whose name and status I didn't ascertain. She informed me that the company had received my letter and invoice, and that they were prepared to pay for the power supply, but not the additional $103.70 for my incurred expenses. I asked her to put any proposals in writing, and I told her I would respond accordingly.

"You don't want us to send you the check now?" she asked. She sounded incredulous that the offer of money was not being gratefully accepted.

I repeated my request for any offer to be sent in writing, and that I would then consider its merits. She agreed to my request, and our conversation concluded without further discussion.

There were several reasons I didn't discuss the offer, or accept it, over the telephone. First, I wanted the details of our dispute on paper, to eliminate any possibility of accidental "memory loss." Second, a quick decision during a brief telephone conversation might be regretted later; considering the written offer at leisure would give me more opportunity to assess its merits. Third, I had corresponded with the president, and a telephone call from an employee whose authority I could not evaluate was not a satisfactory response, although had she offered to settle for the full amount, I would no doubt have gratefully accepted. Finally, my insisting that they go to the trouble of writing to me again increases the possibility they tire of the relentless correspondence, capitulate, and send me a check for the full claim.

If they do send me the full amount, I will of course be pleased to accept it. On the other hand, if the offer is just as described on the telephone and does not include my expenses, I am also prepared to settle for that. I will have had the computer repaired free of charge, which was my main objective, and although I daresay with persistence I might be able to obtain complete settlement, I think their offer is reasonable, and I am prepared to respond in the same vein.

So no matter how many experts advise you that you won't be successful, no matter how daunting the prospects of failure, persistance can and does produce results.

Printed in Canada